USE MIND INSTEAD O▮
TO CHANGE YOUR ▮
BEHAVIOR . . .

"A delightfully unique and eclectic, dog-friendly training book that examines all aspects of maximizing your relationship with your dog."

—Ian Dunbar, Ph.D., MRCVS, Center for
Applied Animal Behavior, author of
How to Teach a New Dog Old Tricks

LOOK AND LISTEN . . .
for the messages your dog is sending to you.

TEACH . . .
your dog—he wants to learn.

PLAY . . .
with your dog—he's bursting with energy and wants
to do it all. Have fun with him.

BE YOUR DOG'S BEST FRIEND

"A well-organized book for thoughtful and discriminating pet owners who enjoy interacting with their dogs. In five minutes of quality time a day, the average dog can become a delightful companion, following the Cantrell program."

—Wendy Volhard, author of *The Holistic
Guide for a Healthy Dog*

━━━━━━━

Krista Cantrell, a cognitive animal behaviorist, is a frequent speaker and clinician in cities nationwide. Her unique no-force training methods grew out of a lifetime spent listening to animals and learning to communicate with them. Over her twenty years of experience, Cantrell has developed her own dog-training philosophy, emphasizing experiential learning and behavior-modification techniques. She lives in the high Sonoran Desert of Arizona with her husband, her two dogs, and five horses.

HOW TO TRAIN ANY DOG IN FIVE MINUTES A DAY

CATCH YOUR DOG DOING SOMETHING RIGHT

Krista Cantrell, M.A.

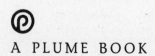

A PLUME BOOK

PLUME
Published by the Penguin Group
Penguin Putnam Inc., 375 Hudson Street
New York, New York 10014, U.S.A.
Penguin Books Ltd, 27 Wrights Lane,
London W8 5TZ, England
Penguin Books Australia Ltd, Ringwood,
Victoria, Australia
Penguin Books Canada Ltd, 10 Alcorn Avenue,
Toronto, Ontario, Canada M4V 3B2
Penguin Books (N.Z.) Ltd, 182–190 Wairau Road,
Auckland 10, New Zealand

Penguin Books Ltd, Registered Offices:
Harmondsworth, Middlesex, England

First published by Plume, an imprint of Dutton Signet,
a member of Penguin Putnam Inc.

First Printing, February, 1998
10 9 8 7 6 5 4 3

playSMART is a registered trademark. Animal Energetics is a
service mark owned by Krista Cantrell.

 REGISTERED TRADEMARK—MARCA REGISTRADA

LIBRARY OF CONGRESS CATALOGING-IN-PUBLICATION DATA

Cantrell, Krista.
    Catch your dog doing something right : how to train any dog in
five minutes a day / Krista Cantrell.
        p.   cm.
    Includes index.
    ISBN 0-452-27755-8
    1. Dogs—Training   I. Title.
SF431.C36   1998
636.7′0835—dc21   97-29692
                                                        CIP

Printed in the United States of America
Set in Stone Serif
Designed by Stanley S. Drate/Folio Graphics Co. Inc.

BOOKS ARE AVAILABLE AT QUANTITY DISCOUNTS WHEN USED TO PROMOTE PRODUCTS OR SERVICES. FOR
INFORMATION PLEASE WRITE TO PREMIUM MARKETING DIVISION, PENGUIN PUTNAM INC., 375 HUDSON
STREET, NEW YORK, NEW YORK 10014.

For Jeff, who makes all things possible.

Contents

ACKNOWLEDGMENTS

Writing is a solitary process. However, writing a book about dogs is a joyous experience because the world of dogs brings together a community of kindred spirits. I would like to thank my teachers, family, friends, and clients for their inspiration, support, and understanding.

A special thanks to Debby Boehm, Kate Kling, Ph.D., and JoAnn White, who saw the book in various stages.

Much gratitude to the following clients and their dogs for appearing in photographs in the book: Stephanie Miller and SeraJoy (Boston terrier), Helen Parkhill and Sunny (Australian shepherd), Darla Waddell and Rocky (Shiba Inu), and Natalie Van der Winner and Molly (German shorthair pointer).

A sincere thank you to Michaela Hamilton, vice president and associate publisher, Dutton Signet; Michael Larson and Elizabeth Pomada, my agents; and Linda Bruce, my assistant.

Most of all, a heartfelt thank you to my husband, Jeff, and to the dogs, especially Amanda, Trevor, and Red Sun Rising C.D.

PREFACE

Two golden retrievers, Trevor and Red Sun Rising, rest at my feet as I write. Occasionally nudging my elbow, they remind me that happy tails, crooked smiles, and willing attitudes are daily gifts with relationships built on patience, understanding, and love. I have learned from Trevor, Red, and their predecessors the following dog handler's creed:

Look at me. Use your eyes to see the messages I am sending you: frantically jumping to greet you when you arrive home after a long day; chewing your leather shoes because they smell like you and the more I chew the softer they get and the better they smell; digging holes so that the cool moist dirt shelters me from the hot noonday sun; or laying tummy up for one more tender scratch.

Teach me. Realize that if I don't come, sit, or stay when you ask me, I am not disobedient; I just don't understand what you want.

Play with me. I am bursting with energy. Fetching balls, catching Frisbees, walking to parks, riding in cars—I love it all.

Be my friend. For that is why my ancestors left the wild to sit by your campfire and share your food. As you accept me, I accept you, completely.

We need each other.

It doesn't matter if your dog is six months old or ten years old, eight pounds or sixty-five pounds, a Chihuahua or a Great Dane, now is the right time to learn new ways to work with your dog. *Catch Your Dog Doing Something Right* shows you how to use your limited time to better advantage by schooling a dog's mind as well as a dog's body.

This book results from my search for new tools and teaching methods based on understanding training from the dog's point of view. Dogs learn in different ways depending on their age, temperament, breed, previous history, and socialization skills. The bodyMIND dog-teaching system described in this book is based on the idea that when dog minds engage, their bodies follow.

When I think about one of the prevalent training methods where handlers are instructed to jerk a choke collar to force a dog to sit, I can understand why there is a huge gap between what handlers want and how dogs respond. From a dog's point of view, there is no obvious causal relationship between pressure on the neck and folding the hindlegs into a sit. Yet, teaching dogs is easy when dogs understand our signals. The problem is we, as handlers, are not clear in what we ask, how we teach, or what dogs need.

Throughout this book you will see the word "handler" instead of "owner." Dogs are my friends. I cannot "own" another being with a mind and feelings distinct from my own. Instead, I choose to share my life with dogs and the responsibilities they bring with them.

Catch Your Dog Doing Something Right provides easy access to the internal mind-set of dogs and how that affects behavior. The book is divided into three sections.

Part 1, "The Search: Discover the Mind in Your Dog's Body," explores how dogs think, process information, and learn. It covers fifteen exercises to determine how a dog learns, and four exercises to understand your influence on the dog's learning process.

Part 2, "The Secret: Catch Your Dog Doing Something Right," describes seven qualities of successful handlers and explains how you can change a dog's behavior with the effective use of your voice, hands, attitude, and signals.

Part 3, "The Plan: Five Minutes a Day," covers how to teach dogs to focus, sit, down, stay, come, stand, and walk. In addition, it shows how to solve behavior problems by using new bodyMIND techniques and short teaching sessions.

The following visual symbols aid your identification of key points, five-minute sessions, ten-second sessions, and help sections.

    KEY POINT

    FIVE-MINUTE SESSION

    TEN-SECOND SESSION

    HELP SECTION

Catch Your Dog Doing Something Right is more than a dog-training manual. It introduces you to a world where dogs think, handlers teach, problems disappear, and happy relationships flourish.

Part 1

THE SEARCH:
Discover the Mind in
Your Dog's Body

CHAPTER 1

STOP, LOOK, LISTEN, SNIFF, AND MOVE:

Exploring the bodyMIND Connection

In Irene Johnson's stack of mail one envelope stood out from all the rest. Irene opened the white linen envelope with the Gilbert town seal on the corner and read in the enclosed letter that she was summoned by the Gilbert prosecutor's office to attend a mediation hearing about her barking dogs. "It must be John, the new neighbor," she thought grimly to herself. "What a troublemaker."

Within seconds she dialed Lorraine, the neighbor who lived on the west side of John's house, to find out if she had received a notice too. In response to her questions, Irene learned that Lorraine had not been summoned to the Gilbert city offices.

Irene's hands shook violently and she banged the tea kettle against the electric burner. Her dogs weren't the only ones that barked; Lorraine's dachshunds barked, so why was she the only one summoned?

During the initial mediation session, Irene learned that the law said it was illegal to harbor an animal who disturbs anyone's peace day or night. John complained that Irene left the Scotties in her backyard from seven in the morning until six-thirty at night. As soon as Irene left in the morning, her Scotties barked continuously for forty to fifty minutes, and then barked at different times throughout the day. Irene explained that John must have included the barking from Lorraine's dachshunds with her Scotties. John said he could tell the difference between the dogs' barks. Besides, Lorraine kept her dachshunds inside the house when she was gone. They only barked if the meter reader came or someone knocked on the door, and then they were quiet.

Behind every bark is a reason. Dogs bark when they are excited, protective, angry, frightened, lonely, anxious, or immature. In order for Irene to solve her dogs' barking problem, she needs to determine why her Scotties bark.

Everytime a dog barks, runs away, chews, digs, cowers, jumps, or bites, you see the result of what the dog thinks. Dogs think—they anticipate, remember, and feel—but most important, they process information and learn.

Car backfires, a hand signal indicating down, an open door, or a visiting cat can provoke a response from a dog. However, a dog's thinking process is more than stimulus and response; more than trial and error. A dog's mind contains a mental system for processing information. Thinking is what a dog engages in between a stimulus and a response.

To understand dog behavior, you need to look through their eyes. Dogs are active learners, not passive learners. Dogs learn about the world from their physical environment and social experiences. As dogs grow up, their ability to discriminate, explore, experiment, and evaluate develops. For example, dogs learn how paws can dig holes and use that knowledge to dig under non-climb-wire fences to escape from fenced yards. Sensitive noses sift through garbage, yet avoid tightly sprung mousetraps. At an early age, dogs learn the difference between hands that tug, pinch, or pull and hands that rub and pet; angry shouts and gentle voices.

As a dog's understanding increases, developing cognitive abilities intervene between events and behaviors. Dogs do not have to react reflexively to chattering squirrels or blaring sirens. Dogs can choose how they respond to different situations. For example, if a squirrel chatters on a high tree branch that a dog cannot reach, a dog can bark excitedly or he can wait quietly in the bushes for the squirrel to leave the safety of the branch. Then, the dog can chase the squirrel on the ground. All dogs act according to what they understand.

Jane Ellen, a German shepherd, is a guide dog for the blind. In that capacity she helps Marvin negotiate stairs, determines the flow of traffic, avoids low-hanging tree branches, and does countless other tasks that require her to effectively evaluate changing conditions. What Jane Ellen knows cannot be reduced completely to previous exposure, since her trainers could not prepare her for every possible contingency. However, her training enabled Jane Ellen to generalize. When confronted with a new situation, Jane Ellen thinks, and acts accordingly.

Behavior is the observable action that enables you to determine a dog's thinking ability. Four factors affect a dog's behavior: (1) the physical environment, (2) a dog's attitude and status, (3) the specific activity, and (4) a handler's influence.

Physical Environment

A dog responds to innate, environmental, and artificial influences. For example, when a dog is hot, he might dig a space in the moist flowerbeds so he can lay down and cool off. The dog does not stop and think, "I'm hot. What can I do about it?" His instinctual response to excessive heat causes him to automatically search for a cool space and dig until he locates cooler dirt. A dog's survival instincts dictate that he keep his body from overheating.

Survival instincts compel a dog to eat when hungry, fight to defend territory, submit when outranked, and flee when in danger. Dogs do not have to be taught how to dig, chase, herd, stalk, attack, bark, or growl; these are instinctual responses.

A dog's life is defined by his immediate vicinity and his position in it. Does the dog live in a crate for eight hours? In a kennel run? Is he tied to a tree? Kept in a basement or a laundry room? Does the dog roam free in the backyard or in the neighborhood? Does a doggy door allow him to go outside at any time?

What can the dog see? Are there windows or sliding-glass doors? Are they covered by curtains or blinds? How much light filters to the dog's quarters? Does the dog live in a dimly lit basement, a dark utility room, a sunny porch, or an airy house?

Does the dog live alone with his handler in a high-rise urban condominium? With children in the suburbs? In a rural area with other animals? Who are his friends or playmates? How many other people, dogs, animals, or children interact with him on a daily basis?

Are the people who live with him neat and tidy or do they leave partially eaten food on counters and tables, drop dirty socks and other clothes on the bedroom carpet, pile newspapers on the kitchen floor, or kick off shoes next to doors and couches? Is there a wastepaper basket without a lid next to the kitchen counter?

The physical environment a dog inhabits affects his behavior. Dogs who live in private and confined quarters often compensate by wild running, barking, and jumping when they are finally set free. Isolated dogs can become timid and fearful or assertive and protective. Messy houses provide dogs with a variety of excuses to nose, sniff, root, eat, or destroy. Where dogs live influences how they respond to visitors, children, other animals, meter readers, and the daily leaving and returning rituals of their handlers. It also contributes to how they behave when left alone or when they encounter new situations.

In addition, dogs react to artificial influences such as sirens, cars, doorbells, car backfires, bicycles, telephones, televisions, radios, stereo systems, trumpets, drums, or any instrument, mechanical device, or piece of equipment that makes noise or moves. For example, a dog might chase a bicycle or a car. When a fire alarm sounds, a dog might howl. When a child practices the saxophone the dog might hide under the bed. How a dog interacts with his world depends on how he views the events that happen.

Dog's Status and Attitude

As puppies, dogs learn the meaning of status. Stronger, bigger puppies get more milk and food than weaker, smaller puppies. Bitches teach their puppies the rules of pack hierarchy with their first action. The mother turns over each puppy and licks them to stimulate the ability to urinate and defecate. The message hidden behind this important physical process is: Mother is dominant. When you meet someone bigger or better than you, roll over and urinate. Eventually, a puppy learns that laying down and wetting also signifies submission. Through his interactions with his mother and packmates, a puppy learns his status, the importance of status, and develops an attitude that corresponds to his position in the pack. A dog's attitude affects his behavior toward his handler, to his fellow packmates, other animals, and toys, as well as his ability to learn.

Whenever I receive a call from someone who has a dog who wets when the person walks in the door, I realize I am dealing with a status issue. For whatever reason, the dog views the person as dominant and automatically urinates. Then, if the person yells at the dog, the urination problem gets worse, since the loud voice reiterates the dominant position of the person.

Eliminating submissive urination requires that the handler find ways to elevate a dog's status, for example, greeting the dog in neutral territory, such as outside in the yard; using a lighter and happier tone of voice; eliminating any reprimand for submissively urinating; and playing confidence-building games with the dog such as tug-of-war and letting the dog win. After a short time the dog accepts his new status and stops wetting.

Specific Activity

Playing ball, catching Frisbees, or moving cattle are activities that build on instincts and drives such as retrieving, herding, or chasing. Other activities such as knocking a phone off the hook and hitting a specific call button to notify police when a medical emergency occurs are not intuitive and require intelligent action by the dog.

Activities that depend on a dog performing a behavior that counters his natural inclinations requires a dog's mind to engage in order to bypass his instincts.

Genoa is a cattle dog whose constant biting at the heels of Cindy and her friends needs to stop. Genoa's herding instincts activate when Cindy or her friends leave one room and go to another area. Genoa follows and nips at their heels. Genoa continues to nip until all the friends are together. To change Genoa's behavior requires that Genoa revise her idea about what is acceptable group behavior. Once Genoa understands that an individual's physical separation from the group is permitted, this new knowledge overrides her instinctual response and the nipping disappears.

Handler Influence

You play a vital role in developing a dog's thinking ability, since a dog's ability to think his way through situations is not an automatic process. As a handler you can work with a dog and help him develop important thinking and listening skills. For example, currently I am working with a one-year-old German shorthair pointer. When I first talked with the handlers, Natalie and Dirk, they described the dog as "uncontrollable." Molly ran constantly around the backyard, jumped on doors, furniture, and people, ignored any signals to come, sit, down, or stay, and disrupted the entire family's routine.

Natalie worried that Molly was too dumb to learn since she had already failed with one trainer. In reality, the problem was that Natalie and Dirk did not know how to channel Molly's natural gifts of running and fetching into acceptable behaviors.

When we talked, I explained that exercise was not enough to stop Molly's constant running, jumping, leaping, or destruction of wooden doors. Molly was in excellent shape. She jogged three miles every day with Dirk and played ball with Natalie for at least one-half hour every day. However, if Molly was required to think, the mental stimulation (mind) would enable Molly to control her own energy naturally and relax (body).

My first task was to teach Natalie, the primary handler, how to increase Molly's ability to focus and pay attention (mind). Then, we could use Molly's love of fetching balls to constructively employ her boundless energy and teach her to come (body). Natalie was skeptical. She played fetch with Molly every day and the dog never got tired. However, when I showed Natalie that she could use those ball playing sessions to teach Molly how to focus and think, Natalie was willing to try. After a short five-minute "think and play ball" session, Molly got physically tired and needed a break.

During our next "think and play ball" session Molly lay down and rested during the session. Natalie was amazed. In later sessions we asked Molly to sit, stay, and wait until Natalie signaled her to fetch the ball. We increased Molly's ability to concentrate and focused her high-energy intensity on making the correct choice.

Molly learned to ignore her instinctual response to run and chase any moving object by learning how to wait and during that pause to focus on Natalie. Learning how to pause gave Molly the short amount of time she needed so that her automatic reactions to run and chase could shut down. The pause enabled Molly to mentally attend to what she should do next. Now, Natalie realizes that Molly is a smart dog who needed to learn how to use her mind, not just her body.

Over time Molly's behavior became more intelligent as a result of well-thought-out teaching sessions that allowed her to build on what she knew and discard what was not useful. In three months Molly changed from uncontrollable wild dog to attentive active dog. Molly comes when called, walks without pulling on the leash, lies quietly inside or outside the house, and no longer chews the doors.

Dogs make decisions constantly. However, when a dog learns to pay attention to you, your input can change a dog's orientation to his environment. Training is a series of cognitive demands. There is a direct link between a dog's inherited abilities, his mind-set (mind), and his behavior (body).

Behavior is an ongoing process because learning is not an isolated event; it happens all the time. How you interact with your dog every time you see him affects how he will respond to you during an official teaching session. If your dog ignores your signals to come when you are inside the house, he will not come to you when he runs loose in the park.

By building on a dog's natural awareness, you can increase his perception beyond the physical or instinctual. A bodyMIND approach enables dogs to bypass instincts, pay attention to handlers, and ignore competing environmental events.

A dog acts out what he thinks. As the dog learns new ideas, his behavior changes. It is the difference between a dog who barks at the doorbell as a reflexive action and a dog who noses a hearing-impaired person's hand when the doorbell rings.

Working with a dog's mind is the missing link in creating extraordinary relationships and solving inappropriate behaviors.

CHAPTER 2

A DOG IS A DOG,
IS A DOG,
IS A DOG . . .

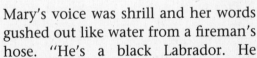

Mary's voice was shrill and her words gushed out like water from a fireman's hose. "He's a black Labrador. He should be part duck, but he refuses to swim. He won't even walk in the wading pool. When I put him in the swimming pool, he sinks like a stone; he doesn't even try to move his legs. He can't be afraid of water. I've had Labradors for fifteen years and no purebred Lab refuses to swim. Can you help me?"

There are many people like Mary who believe that all Labradors swim, all cocker spaniels are friendly, all Saint Bernards move slowly, all greyhounds chase rabbits, all rottweilers are protective, and all pit bulls are dangerous. However, Mary is wrong. Although every dog who belongs to a specific breed has similar characteristics, identical dogs do not exist. Dogs are unique individuals with differing physical, mental, and emotional abilities.

To understand landlocked Labradors, timid Doberman pinschers, unfriendly cocker spaniels, retrievers who do not fetch, and pointers who refuse to hunt birds, we need to go back in time to the beginning of the dog-human relationship to look for clues.

The first dogs were probably wolves, jackals, or wild dogs who followed hunters when they pursued game and snatched at the remains. As time passed, they chose to live with hunters and their families. It was a natural step to move from the back of the hunt to the front where they could flush out game for the hunters to kill.

All dogs share these ancestors, but over the years specific breeds were developed to accentuate certain characteristics such as the ability to stand and point out rabbits, retrieve pheasants, or burrow after badgers. In addition, dogs were bred to perform jobs such as guarding sheep, killing rats, or protecting family members.

Dogs are distinguished by their keen senses of smell, sight, hearing, and perception—important survival traits in any situation. They can hear ultrasonic vibrations, recognize minute facial expressions, follow movement easily, and discern mood changes. They can smell drugs, find trapped people, detect gas leaks, locate game, pull a sled, and act as guide dogs. There are search-and-rescue dogs, hearing-assistance dogs, therapy dogs, protection dogs, show dogs, hunting dogs, and companions.

Dogs play different roles in today's contemporary lifestyles. In the past, pointers daily trudged through weeds, grass, and water to flush out game in order to provide a family's meals. Terriers were ferocious mousers who killed mice so that people might live in rodent-free homes. Today, performance requirements for most dogs have changed. Although we still want search-and-rescue dogs, hunting dogs, guide dogs, and protection dogs, the major role for most dogs is that of companion.

This change from a performance-based standard produces dogs who cannot swim, scent game, or hear. As a result, some dogs have lost the special traits or physical capabilities that were developed and passed on through generations of selective breeding. To find a healthy performance dog contact a breeder who raises dogs that participate in hunting tests or field trials, lure coursing, earth dog events, herding, agility, or obedience. Every dog can perform. However, the challenge you face is to discover a particular dog's bodyMIND learning style.

Dogs dig, growl, bark, run away, submissively urinate, and perform countless other behaviors at inappropriate times when they have not been treated as animals who think. Dogs anticipate, remember, and feel, but most important, they think. Every time you see a dog come when called, chase a cat, or execute a perfect sit-stay in an obedience show ring, you see the results of what the dog thinks.

You teach dogs to use their minds because you know someday you and your dog will be in a situation where his instincts will want to take over. If you just train the dog's body, when his instincts surface he will respond to those drives. If you teach a dog to think, he will listen to you in spite of his instincts. You play a vital role in your dog's learning process. bodyMIND learning does not happen automatically; it must be nurtured.

In order to increase a dog's ability to think his way through any situation, you must create learning experiences that reward a dog for using his mind instead of following his instincts. When a dog is encouraged to think, he starts a learning process that carries over into everything he does.

Just like people who work better when praised for their efforts instead of being "constructively" criticized, dogs learn faster with rewards. Rewards strengthen a correct response. They teach dogs that they made the right choice.

Too many people still believe that reward is the absence of punishment. However, if a dog does not recognize the specific action he performed that avoided punishment, he cannot easily repeat a desired behavior. Guiding, rather than compelling or forcing, a dog's behavior requires a complete rethinking of the dog/handler relationship. The lessons you design must build a dog's confidence in himself, in you as the handler, and in your relationship.

Your job is to provide the appropriate reward, at the right time, so dogs can choose correctly. Dogs start learning when they make choices based on information you give them. They learn quickly that rewards are not arbitrary but hinge on their response.

By evaluating a dog's cognitive abilities you can base your teaching program on a dog's aptitude and interests. For Jack, the handler of Rose, a sensitive borzoi, understanding his dog's mind and learning capabilities meant the difference between a happy home and a one-way trip to the local humane society for his Rose.

As a puppy, Rose was very withdrawn. As an adult dog, Rose, although sweet, was aloof and slept all day on the couch. Rose cringed and cowered when Jack yelled at her to come or wanted her to play inside the house.

Jack called me because he was completely frustrated with Rose's response to him. Jack wanted a pal, a friend, a buddy, and Rose refused to play with him. Yet, she ran, chased rabbits, and menaced any stray dogs who happened to enter the yard. Through the *PAR* (*P*ower, *A*ctivity, and *R*esponse) exercises, Jack learned why his loud masculine voice threatened Rose and how he could motivate Rose to play with, not hide from, him.

PAR stands for mental *P*ower level, physical *A*ctivity level, and emotional *R*esponse level. These three factors help handlers understand how dogs react, think, and learn. In addition, they indicate a dog's willingness to perform. The PAR exercises enable you to determine a dog's suitability for a particular teaching format or lifestyle. The PAR approach requires that you observe your dog's actions in specific exercises and assess it objectively. Then, you can avoid using labels like dumb, hyperactive, or neurotic that prevent you from seeing solutions.

Handlers teach by using their voice, legs, hands, body position, and mind. However, dog handlers get trapped. They perform the same actions over and over even when the dog does not respond correctly. Then, when the dog does not perform, the handler's frustration escalates. The PAR approach decreases handler frustration by increasing your understanding of a dog's bodyMIND attitude and how it affects learning.

Chapter 3 contains fifteen PAR exercises that show you the link between your dog's mind and his behavior, and four exercises that indicate your influence on a dog's learning process.

When dogs learn that making the right choice earns rewards, they have a reason to pay attention to you and not focus on joggers, bikers, or stray cats. With their ability to think, they become happy, self-confident dogs who want to be caught doing something right.

CHAPTER **3**

HOW EASILY DO DOGS LEARN?

Fifteen Exercises to Understand a Dog's Mind and Four Exercises to Understand Your Influence

Anatomy lessons are powerful. Standing in front of full-length mirrors that act as closet doors, I face myself every morning and evening. Even a casual glance reminds me of the subtle message that bodies send:

Two eyes to see; watch more than talk.
Two ears to hear; listen more than speak.
Two legs to run, jump, and skip; play more than work.
Two arms to hold, touch, and guide; embrace more than scold.
One mouth; think before words escape lips.

We want dogs to recognize words and phrases such as "no," "good girl," "go to your bed," "do you need to go out?" that ask in a whisper or command in a shout. We require dogs to know that joggers are not quickly escaping prey, dinnertime is not an excuse to beg, and gardens are for flowers, not for digging. We expect dogs to understand without any notice or warning if we are happy, tired, crabby, angry, sad, or lonely. Our expectations are much greater than sit, down, stay, come, and heel.

In order for dogs to live comfortably in our world, we need to learn how dogs communicate and understand their unique physical and mental gifts. Dogs express themselves by movements as small as a flick of the ear or as big as a full body-slam greeting. Every time dogs act, you see the results of what they think. Mind exists in a dog's body.

Handlers often fail to solve problems because they forget to ask questions about what dogs think and feel. The PAR exercises allow you to look past the reflection in the mirror, examine the dog's world, and change your assumptions about dog behavior.

Many people actually ignore large parts of a dog's behavior once they label the problem. For example, Dana came to my office with a three-year-old beagle, Chez. During the past week Chez had growled at joggers and threatened to bite two people in the park. On the phone Dana described Chez as nervous and stressed. She said that Chez would not follow food lures or accept food rewards in her office. Yet the first time I rewarded Chez with food, she gobbled it down. Chez continued to eat her rewards during the entire session. We worked on focus, sit, down, walk by my side, and come with complete success. Chez, sat, laid down, walked happily with a food lure, came, and even jumped on my lap for touching.

When I asked Dana her opinion of Chez's behavior, she described Chez as stressed because her tail was not up. I pointed out that although Chez's tail was not completely upright, it was held away from her body and not tucked tight through her back legs. I reminded Dana that the breeders sold Chez because she carried her tail low in the show ring.

Dana was so busy concentrating on Chez's tail that she did not see the happy footsteps, the eager approach to a stranger (me), or how quickly Chez learned to sit and down. Dana had labeled Chez as stressed and nervous and ignored other behaviors that contradicted the label.

PAR exercises do not label a dog as good, bad, dumb, or brilliant. Instead, they indicate a dog's preferred bodyMIND learning style and his weaker learning skills. Armed with that knowledge you can determine the best way to teach a dog new behaviors and the easiest way to change inappropriate habits.

PAR exercises enable you to evaluate your dog's intelligent behavior in different situations. Then, you can know what to expect when your dog experiences something new such as a hot-air balloon landing in front of him, a stray cat wandering through the neighbor's rosebushes, or your request for a sit-stay in a hotel lobby. The exercises are not a personality test. Rather, they are a test of the dog's physical, mental, and emotional abilities; and ability exercises are a better predictor of future responses and actions.

Fifteen PAR exercises help you understand how dogs

learn. Mental *Power* level exercises explore dog aware-ness and thought process. Physical *Activity* level exer-cises indicate which senses dogs favor, as well as what interests and motivates them. Emotional *Response* level exercises demonstrate how dogs perceive, receive, and share different emotional states. Each exercise exam-ines one particular facet of a dog's bodyMIND ap-proach. However, all the learning variables are interdependent. For example, confidence is different than trust. However, when a dog's confidence is low, it affects a dog's ability to trust.

Four PAR exercises enable you to assess your influ-ence on the dog's learning process. Attraction-to-handler exercises demonstrate the amount of attraction between you and your dog. Effect-of-handler-attitude exercises show how what you feel affects your dog's per-formance.

These exercises should not be interpreted as perma-nent indicators of a dog's learning ability, since learn-ing is an ongoing process. Do not label your dog for life because of the results! Dogs change and the exercises change the dogs. If you evaluate a dog before you work with him, then examine him after you have practiced Animal Energetics techniques for a month and the dog has learned to focus, sit, and down; the dog will re-spond differently.

Whether you conduct the exercises inside or out-side, plan them when no other animals, children, adults, or other distractions are present. Schedule them before the dog eats. Do not allow them to interfere with a regularly scheduled event such as your daughter arriv-ing home from school. A dog's PAR performance depends on his age, health, physical condition, time of day, season, and previous experience with PAR tests.

Each exercise takes five minutes or less. Instructions describe the amount of preparation time, location, and equipment needed. If you cannot find a specific item, improvise. Use your imagination and find a substitute that serves the same purpose and is safe for the dog. After you complete each exercise, circle the best description of the dog's response.

The PAR exercises require patience on the part of the handler. Do not perform more than five exercises at one time. If the dog seems tired after two or three exercises, stop. Continue with the exercises at another time. Work with only one dog at a time and observe the dog's approach, reactions, and response to you. Look for specific physical actions, except barking. Although barking is a vocal response it is not always a good indicator of what the dog actually thinks. Instead, observe a dog's body language and examine his behavior; then you can uncover how what a dog thinks directs his actions. Remember, there is no such thing as a poor performance.

When you conduct an exercise outside, if you are not inside a fenced yard, attach a long leash or a twenty-foot lightweight rope to the dog's collar so that if something else grabs the dog's attention he cannot go to it. Do not ever use the leash to drag the dog into position.

Dogs can choose from a variety of behaviors, and a dog's decision to choose a specific action is directed by what he knows. Intelligent behavior intervenes before and during events. The PAR exercises indicate the type of exchange that occurs between you and your dog and between your dog and other events. Allow the PAR exercises to serve as a guide so you can understand your dog's bodyMIND attitude and adapt your teaching style and expectations to the dog. Then, it will be easier for you to teach a dog new habits and solve behavior problems.

If you have a territorial, aggressive, or protective dog modify the activities accordingly or do not perform them. You do not want your dog to attack, bite, scare anyone, or be scared. Seek professional assistance in working with such a dog.

Five Mental Power Level Exercises

The Mental Power Level indicates how dogs' mental characteristics influence what they attend to and how they process information in the presence of something new or altered in their environment.

ATTENTION SPAN

PREPARATION TIME: 0 minutes
LOCATION: Inside
EQUIPMENT: No equipment needed

Call the dog's name in a happy cheerful voice. Does the dog flick an ear, turn his head, angle his body to see you, come to you, or ignore you? Once the dog looks at you, how long can you keep the dog's attention by using your voice? squeaking a toy? bouncing a ball? waving a food treat?

Circle the best description of the dog's attention span for each item.

- Long: more than thirty seconds
- Medium: ten to thirty seconds
- Short: less than ten seconds
- No response

IMPLICATIONS FOR TEACHING

Dogs with long attention spans learn after a few repetitions and can work for longer periods of time without needing a break. Avoid the temptation to teach dogs with long attention spans everything in one day.

Dogs with medium attention spans may need some reminding the next day after you teach them, but they learn after a moderate number of repetitions. Use five-minute schooling sessions to build the dog's excitement in you. Act enthusiastic during lesson time and watch the dog's attention quadruple!

Dogs with short attention spans often need many repetitions to learn something because their attention scatters easily. Frequent ten-second teaching sessions are excellent ways to teach and repeat what you want the dog to learn while maintaining the dog's interest. Teaching the dog to focus will challenge your ability to invent new ways to use food, toys, balls, and activity motivators to sustain the dog's attention. Be patient. Eventually, the dog's attention span will increase.

MEMORY

PREPARATION TIME: 1 minute

LOCATION: Inside

EQUIPMENT: Dog toy, dog dish with food, towel, or blanket

Play with the dog using his favorite toy. When the dog is happy and excited, stop playing. While the dog watches, hide the toy under a large towel or small blanket. Does the dog search for his toy?

HELP

If your dog does not play with toys but likes food, place a small amount of the dog's favorite food or treat in his dog dish. Hold the dish out to the dog and let him eat one mouthful from it. Then, hide the dish under the towel.

Circle the best description of the dog's ability member where the toy or treat is hidden.

- Paws and nuzzles for the toy or treat until he finds it
- Paws and gives up
- Waits and watches
- Forgets about it and leaves the area
- No response

Repeat this exercise. Does the dog take less time to figure out where the item is after you hide it a second time?

IMPLICATIONS FOR TEACHING

Dogs with long memories can remember from one teaching session to the next. They often need to perform an exercise only once or twice and then they know it. An added benefit is that during schooling sessions you can practice many different exercises and the dog does not get confused.

Dogs with medium memories may start and stop, or wait and watch. They do not usually tie two separate actions together. In this exercise the dogs may realize that the toy is under the blanket, but they do not recognize that in order to recover it they must keep pawing and searching. Dogs with moderate memories need prompting to stay on task. Verbal reminders such as "that's what I want," "over here," "this way," and "faster" guide a dog to complete an activity.

Dogs with short memories forget quickly. In the middle of a schooling session they act as if they have

The toy is placed on the floor between us. JEFF CANTRELL

I encourage Red to find the toy under the towel. JEFF CANTRELL

Red searches for the toy. JEFF CANTRELL

Red finds the toy and carries it away. JEFF CANTRELL

no idea of what is happening. For example, they run to get the ball, drop it, and go somewhere else. Frequently, they do not remember the previous day's lesson. Dividing a behavior into smaller and smaller parts helps dogs with short memories to stay on task. For example, first practice getting the dog to take the ball from your hand and then release it to you. Next, have the dog pick the ball up on the floor in front of him and give it to you. Then, teach the dog to find the ball when it is a short distance away and bring it to you. Finally, ask the dog to fetch a tossed ball and return it to you.

CONCENTRATION

PREPARATION TIME: 1 minute.
LOCATION: Choose a quiet outside location
EQUIPMENT: Toys, balls, treats, dog leash

Before you take the dog on a walk in the yard, place a few dog toys, favorite snacks, balls, or other items on the ground in different locations. Walk the dog through the "distractions." Does the dog touch the items with his nose, grab them with his teeth, or walk right past them? Does the dog ignore some items and not others?

Circle the best description of the dog's ability to ignore the distractions.

- Ignores the items
- Sniffs at the items and walks by
- Grabs or eats only certain items
- Grabs or eats each item as soon as he sees it

IMPLICATIONS FOR TEACHING

Dogs who consistently concentrate and focus on the handler without any teaching are rare. Most dogs are distracted by different items and events. The purpose of schooling dogs is to teach them to focus on you, since dogs who do not watch their handlers are at a learning disadvantage.

This exercise shows you what attracts your dog's attention; use it to your best advantage. If a dog ignores the food, but grabs the balls, use balls as the dog's primary motivator or reward. If a dog ignores the toys but eats the food, use food as his primary motivator or reward during your teaching sessions. If a dog ignores the items on the ground, try different distractions such as children playing, a bicycle lying on its side, other animals, or someone bouncing a ball so you can learn what attracts your dog's attention.

When you are aware of what distracts your dog, you can prepare for those contingencies by developing different schooling sessions geared to focus a dog's attention to you in spite of the presence of potential distractions. Dogs who concentrate on their handlers give handlers more flexibility in when, where, and how they work.

REASONING

PREPARATION TIME: 1 minute

LOCATION: Choose a quiet outside location

EQUIPMENT: Tree, fence post, or column, a long leash or rope, toy, treat, ball, or food

Find a sturdy tree, fence post, or column in the yard that you can loop a leash around one time. (Tie a knot so it is secure or run the fastener end of the leash through the loop end and create a slip knot.) Fasten the dog to the leash and stand one foot beyond his reach. Call the dog. If the dog does not try to come to you, use food treats, balls, or toys as incentives. For one minute encourage the dog to reach you. Does the dog figure out that if he goes around to the other side of the tree, he can unwrap the leash and reach you?

Circle the best description of the dog's reasoning ability.

- Goes to the other side of the tree, which unwraps the leash, and comes to you
- Constantly pulls to reach you, but does not unwrap the leash
- Pulls to reach you, then stops and waits
- Watches and waits, no pulling
- No response

IMPLICATIONS FOR TEACHING

Dogs who unwrap the leash from around the tree after a short delay show great flexibility in their thought process. These dogs initiate actions without any guidance and modify their behavior according to context. These "take-charge" dogs adapt easily to new environments. They learn quickly but need effective leadership or they will follow their plans instead of yours.

Dogs who unwrap the leash from around the tree after a medium or long delay also indicate flexibility in their thought process. Although slower, their reasoning ability still enables them to modify their behavior successfully once the information about their current situation percolates through. The fact that these dogs persist and resolve this problem successfully bodes well for handlers who are attentive to the times when dogs look to their handlers for additional guidance and information. Dogs who pause, then act, learn with just a little handler assistance, and adapt without much difficulty to new environments.

Dogs who do not unwrap the leash but struggle or wait patiently have limited flexibility. The situation they find themselves in binds them. Context-bound dogs need guidance if they are to adapt to new situations.

PROBLEM SOLVING

PREPARATION TIME: 3 minutes
LOCATION: Inside
EQUIPMENT: A dogproof barrier

Create a four-foot-long barrier by using a baby gate, cardboard boxes, a towel strung out between two chairs, or a row of chairs with low chair rungs that prevent a dog from going under the chairs. Place one side of the barrier against a wall. Leave the other side open so the dog can go around it. Stand in the middle behind the barrier. Call the dog a few times. Use an excited, enthusiastic, happy voice. If the dog does not try to come to you, use food treats, balls, or toys as incentives. For one minute encourage the dog to reach you. How long does it take the dog to find the open end?

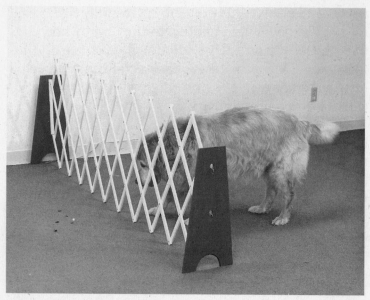

Trevor behind the barrier. JEFF CANTRELL

Trevor figures out how to go around the barrier. JEFF CANTRELL

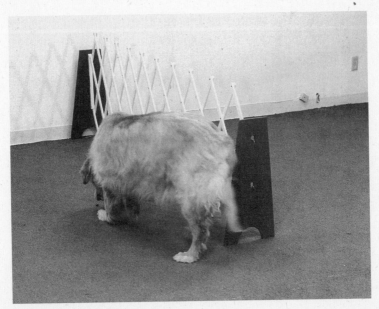

Trevor eats the food. JEFF CANTRELL

After the dog figures out how to reach you, create an opening at the other end by moving the barrier one foot away from the wall. Then, block the formerly open end so that if the dog goes there he cannot get through. Stand in the middle behind the barrier. Call the dog. Does the dog take less time or more time to figure out where the new opening is?

Circle the best description of the dog's problem-solving ability.

- Immediately, within ten seconds, finds the open end and comes
- After a short pause, between ten and thirty seconds, comes
- Slowly, between thirty seconds and two minutes, comes
- Jumps the barrier or knocks it over
- Stops in front of the barrier and waits
- Leaves the area
- No response

HELP
If the dog does not respond to your voice, place a small amount of the dog's favorite food or treat in his dog dish. Hold the dish out to the dog and let him eat one mouthful from it. Then, place the dish behind the barrier where he can see it.

IMPLICATIONS FOR TEACHING

Dogs who immediately find the open side, as well as dogs who jump the barrier, are highly creative in their approach. Their curiosity and investigative nature enable them to adapt easily to a variety of situations. They do not give up when they have a goal in mind and make "plans." These dogs are the ones who figure out that if they push the chair next to the kitchen counter they can use it to jump up and eat the cake left sitting on the counter. They are quick to learn and eventually solve all problems that come their way. Challenge their interest during schooling sessions by asking them to do the same things but in new ways. For example, teach them to walk in a figure eight between two trees, two cones, and then between your legs.

Dogs who stop in front of the barrier, wait, and give up often stop trying during schooling sessions if things seem too difficult or complicated. Dividing an activity into smaller parts helps dogs avoid becoming overwhelmed by too much information or the need to make too many decisions. Consistency, doing the same thing, at the same time, in the same way, aids a passive dog's ability to learn new things.

Dogs who leave the area or refuse to try are not stimulated by challenges and do not indicate a strong attraction to you or to any of the motivators. Future schooling sessions must build the dog's sense of adventure, excitement about new things, and interest in you so that he responds willingly.

Five Physical Activity Level Exercises

The Physical Activity Level indicates how dogs' physical senses influence what they attend to and how they process information, as well as what interests and motivates them in the presence of something new or altered in their environment.

MOVEMENT

PREPARATION TIME: 1 minute
LOCATION: Inside
EQUIPMENT: String, favorite toy, unfamiliar object

Tie a string to your dog's favorite toy. Drag and bounce it along the floor. Does the dog chase it, watch it, ignore it, or hide from it? If the dog was attracted to it, drag something that the dog has never played with before like a children's toy on a rope. Watch the dog's reaction. Does it change?

Circle the best description of the dog's response to movement.

- Chases
- Chases and pounces
- Follows at a distance
- Watches and investigates
- Watches and remains motionless
- Backs away
- No response

IMPLICATIONS FOR TEACHING

Dogs who chase and investigate, come close and watch, but do not bite or snap as you drag the toy are active dogs who get excited easily. When you school an eager dog, remember these high-energy dogs give 150 percent all the time. Use fewer gestures, act calmly, and be ready for a big response. Eager dogs love play activities with movement. Teaching "come" turns into a great game for an eager dog; once you get the dog's attention, moving backwards, away from the dog, builds on his natural instinct to chase.

Dogs who chase and pounce, crowd the handler, or snap or bite at the toy or the handler's feet are extremely active dogs who get overexcited easily. When you school bold dogs, remember they often overreact to any motion they see. Avoid any large, dramatic, or showy gestures or movements. Channel the bold dog's exuberance into play activities that ask him to think first, then respond. For example, you ask the dog to sit and wait *before* he fetches the tennis ball.

Dogs who watch and remain motionless, follow at a distance, or run or back away as you drag the toy are low-involvement dogs who, because they are uncertain of what will happen next, maintain very cautious and "safe" positions. They leave enough space between you and them so they can escape quickly if necessary. When you school cautious dogs, remember that they are wary of unexpected events. Avoid scaring these dogs by surprising them. Usually cautious dogs play in response to what you initiate. However, they may hesitate if the play activities become too rambunctious. When they feel "safe," though, they can be fairly active. Teaching cautious dogs requires that you design schooling sessions and find locations where they can feel secure.

Indifferent dogs are extremely inactive. They ignore what goes on and rarely respond to anything. Check to make sure that the dog is not sick. Indifferent dogs can either be easy or difficult dogs to work with depending on their PAR approach to learning. They do not respond well to play activities as motivators, but sometimes food or squeak toys focus their attention. Teach the dog how to listen, focus on you, and respond with a little excitement before you teach the dog a behavior such as come that asks them to move.

SIGHT

PREPARATION TIME: 1 minute

LOCATION: Inside

EQUIPMENT: Large paper grocery or shopping bag, large sheet, another person

Play with your dog. After a few minutes ask someone to hold the dog while you walk to the other side of the room. Tell the person to release the dog once you call her name. Place a paper bag over your head. Call the dog.

On another occasion cover yourself from head to toe with a sheet. Then, call the dog.

Circle the best description of the dog's sight sensitivity.

- Immediately comes to you
- Hesitates and then comes
- Searches but does not find you

- Backs away or leaves the room
- No response

IMPLICATIONS FOR TEACHING

Dogs who depend on what they see to make decisions frequently do not find the "hidden" handler. They might search and not find you, back away, or leave the room. Sight-dominant dogs pay attention to

Red comes in spite of the bag over my head. JEFF CANTRELL

the smallest visual changes, which is a training advantage since you can alter your body posture slightly or use a small gesture and they notice it immediately. Be aware that what these dogs see affects their response. For example, a dog may not come to you when you wear sunglasses. Or a dog might bark at one of your friends if she wears a large hat, carries shopping bags, or walks in with an open umbrella. Be prepared for a sight-dependent dog to respond immediately to any visual changes. In addition, recognize that the response may be opposite of what you want.

Dogs who do not depend on what they see to make decisions usually find the "hidden" handler. Although some dogs may hesitate, many dogs run immediately to the handler. Dogs who are not sight dominant depend more on one of their other senses to aid them in their decision making.

SOUND

> *PREPARATION TIME:* 1 minute
> *LOCATION:* Inside
> *EQUIPMENT:* Something to make loud noises with, another person

When you and the dog are together inside the house, have someone outside the house make loud and unusual noises with items such as metal pans banging against each other, metal garbage can lids striking against each other, or musical instruments playing sounds the dog has never heard before. Does the dog hide, become uneasy, seek your attention, or ignore the noises?

Ask the person creating the noise to come inside and make more noise in another room of the house. Does the dog respond differently depending on whether the noise is outside or inside?

Circle the best description of the dog's response to noise outside and inside the house.

- Extremely noise sensitive
- Fairly noise sensitive
- Little or no response

IMPLICATIONS FOR TEACHING

This exercise explores a dog's reaction to noise from objects. However, it does not test a dog's sensitivity to nature sounds such as rainstorms and lightning, or human noises such as yelling. Noise sensitivity varies depending on the dog, the type of noise, the intensity of the sound, and its position relative to the dog.

Dogs who react intensely to loud or unusual outside noises can have three very different reactions. They can run toward the noise, run away, or hide. Dogs who are extremely noise sensitive experience high stress daily through normal city sounds such as police sirens, fire alarms, loud mufflers, or car backfires. If a dog is extremely noise sensitive, play soft music on the radio, close shutters, blinds, or curtains, bring the dog inside, and practice Animal Energetics to relieve his tension.

Dogs who react moderately to loud or unusual noises may seek out the source of the noise, bark, but stop on their own and calm down after a short amount of time. Dogs who are fairly noise sensitive often respond positively when you use whistles, clapping, or other mildly enthusiastic noises during schooling sessions.

Dogs who react barely or not at all to loud or unusual noises may not respond for two very different reasons. They either ignore the loud or unusual noises because they are mellow dogs, or they are hard-of-hearing or deaf. Dogs who are not noise sensitive depend more on one of their other senses to aid them in their decisions.

TOUCH

PREPARATION TIME: 0 minutes
LOCATION: Inside
EQUIPMENT: No equipment required

Touch, stroke, and rub the dog while he lays down on the floor. How long can you touch him? Can you touch him anywhere? On his stomach, back, neck, shoulders, tail, paws, face? Can you lift up his lips to look at his teeth? Does he roll over on his back when you touch him or raise a paw to you? Does he bump your hand with his nose when you stop touching? Does he bark, growl, or bite at you or your hand to tell you not to touch him?

Circle the best description of the dog's response to touching.

- Allows touching everywhere on his body
- Can only be touched in certain areas
- Avoids touching
- Snaps, growls, or bites to prevent touching

IMPLICATIONS FOR TEACHING

Dogs who accept physical contact anywhere on their bodies are usually quite adaptable. Sometimes they are less outgoing, but they are normally easy to teach.

Dogs who accept physical contact in some areas but not all usually have at least one current or potential behavior problem. Dogs store tension in their bodies. Areas that cannot be touched indicate where dogs store their stress. Practicing Animal Energetics relieves the stress that causes a dog to shy away from physical contact. For example, dogs who are afraid of thunderstorms often do not like their hindquarters touched. After a few months of Animal Energetics sessions dogs will accept touching and are no longer afraid of thunder.

Dogs who resist physical contact are frequently difficult to teach. They might be afraid of your touch or exceedingly dominant, which causes them to oppose your touch. If a dog snaps, growls, or bites to prevent touching, seek professional help.

TASTE/SMELL

PREPARATION TIME: 2 minutes
LOCATION: Inside
EQUIPMENT: Food treats

When your dog is out of the room, lay a food treat trail and see if your dog follows it. Does the dog start sniffing as soon as he enters the room and locates each morsel of food? Does he even notice the food treats? Does he ignore the treats and come to you? Try using different types of food treats such as dry dog biscuits, cheese, freeze-dried liver, or beef jerky to see if that changes your dog's response.

Circle the best description of the dog's response to taste/smell.

- Eats the food instantly and follows the trail
- Sniffs the food and leaves it
- Ignores the food

IMPLICATIONS FOR TEACHING

This exercise is a great way to find out the extent to which food motivates your dog.

Dogs who immediately search out the food and follow the trail are extremely food/smell driven. They respond well when food is used as a motivator for teaching sit, down, or stand. Food can be used as a reward with excellent results.

Dogs who sniff food and leave it because they would rather be with you demonstrate a high degree of handler or social attraction. They respond well when "you" are the reward, such as touching, play time, or activity motivators that involve games with you. For example, teaching "come" to these dogs is easier because they come to "you."

Dogs who ignore food and do not search you out during this exercise will not view food or time spent with you as a reward for their efforts. Instead, look to other motivators such as balls, toys, games, or activities to inspire them to action. Frequently, this type of dog is quite independent and motivates with great difficulty.

Emotional Response Level

The Emotional Response Level indicates how dogs perceive, receive, and share different emotional states in the presence of something new or altered in their environment.

EXCITABILITY

PREPARATION TIME: 0 minute
LOCATION: Inside
EQUIPMENT: An unfamiliar person

Ask someone to ring the doorbell and knock on the door. How does the dog react? Next, invite the person inside the house. How does the dog greet the person? How long does it take for the dog to settle down?

Circle the best description of the dog's emotional response.

- Charges at the door
- Runs to the door
- Keeps a short distance from the door
- Hides or retreats to a different room
- No response

Circle the best description of the dog's greeting of the person.

- Runs up, circles the person, or jumps on him
- Watches, but does not come up
- Hides behind you or something in the room
- Retreats to a different room
- No response

How long does it take for the dog to settle down?

- Immediately: less than ten seconds
- After a short pause: between ten and thirty seconds
- Slowly: between thirty seconds and two minutes
- More than two minutes

IMPLICATIONS FOR TEACHING

This exercise only assesses the impact of a sound, the doorbell and knocking, and the presence of an unfamiliar person. However, dogs who do not react in this situation might become very excited when they are outside and see another dog, a jogger, children, a bicyclist, or a stranger. Take five minutes and think about your dog. Then, design schooling sessions appropriate for his needs.

Dogs who run to the door, interact with, jump on, or circle the person are very outgoing, seek attention, and get excited easily. During schooling sessions do not repeat the same exercise over and over again. When you practice Animal Energetics move your hand quickly and place it in different locations to keep their attention focused. Teaching stay often is a challenge with dogs who get excited easily since they want to constantly explore, inspect, and interact. The key is to focus their attention on you at all times.

Dogs who charge the door and the person or nip or bite at feet are extremely extroverted, demand attention, and get overexcited easily. With bold dogs, school time happens all day long. To reinforce the idea that you are the teacher and the dog is the student, always walk through doorways first; do not step around the dog but ask the dog to move out of your way; eat first, then let the dog eat; and make the dog earn attention from you by asking him to sit, down, or stand before you touch or feed him. The key with bold dogs is for you to stay calm and stay in charge. Then, teaching sit, down, come, stay, stand, or walk by your side goes smoothly.

Dogs who watch and wait or keep a short distance from the door and the person are friendly dogs who welcome attention when they feel safe and act excited when encouraged. They are eager to please and just need a little help getting started. Teaching any activity that requires waiting quietly such as stay is easy. However, if their hesitation turns into wariness, they require different handling. Dogs who hide behind you or a piece of furniture or retreat to a different room can be unpredictable if cornered. They accept attention when it is not perceived as a threat, but any excitement often stresses them. These dogs need support and specific schooling sessions to build their confidence. Avoid scaring them by surprising them without notice or changing the rules. They can be extremely outgoing with people they know and quite timid with strangers. Introducing them to different people and events in nonthreatening ways can build their trust.

Dogs who ignore the sound of the doorbell, knocking, and the presence of a stranger avoid attention, do not get excited easily, and are very retiring. Depending on their attitude they can either be easy or difficult dogs to work with. If a dog does not respond, check that he is not sick and try a different "sound" event. During schooling sessions spend your time building the dog's interest in you and in his environment.

The amount of time it takes dogs to stop bouncing, charging, or hiding and to relax is a good indication of their intensity. Dogs whose reaction increases or who calm down with difficulty need schooling sessions that teach them how to listen, wait, pause, and relax. Dogs whose response diminishes almost immediately or after a short pause respond positively to enthusiasm and lessons that emphasize active participation.

CONFIDENCE

PREPARATION TIME: 3 minutes
LOCATION: Inside
EQUIPMENT: ''Tunnel,'' another person

Ask your dog to go through a tunnel. Tunnels can be everything from children's plastic play tunnels, to cardboard boxes that are open on both ends, to chairs or tables with a sheet draped over them to cover the sides. The tunnel should be at least three times as long as the dog's body. Check that there are at least three inches between the dog's shoulders and the top of the tunnel. Have a friend hold your dog at one end of the tunnel. Rest on your knees at the other end, tap the bottom of the tunnel, and call the dog's name. Does the dog come to you instantly, with hesitation, or refuse to come?

Circle the best description of the dog's confidence.

- Enters the tunnel and comes out the other end
- Hesitates, enters the tunnel, and comes out the other end

Red easily enters the tunnel. JEFF CANTRELL

Red runs out of the end of the tunnel. JEFF CANTRELL

- Hesitates, enters the tunnel, stops, and backs out
- Refuses to enter the tunnel

HELP
If the dog does not come when you call, wave the dog's favorite food treat or squeak a special toy at the other end of the tunnel.

IMPLICATIONS FOR TEACHING

Dogs who enter the tunnel and come out the other end usually approach new or unusual settings with the same degree of confidence. Schooling sessions can introduce new situations and exercises faster because these dogs adapt quickly.

Dogs who hesitate, enter the tunnel, stop, and back out often face other situations with a similar lack of resolution to continue if tasks are perceived as too big. Schooling sessions must divide activities into smaller parts to help dogs avoid becoming overwhelmed by too much information or the need to make too many decisions. These dogs need reassurance and prompting to stay on task.

Dogs who refuse to enter the tunnel may choose not to enter for two very different reasons. They either refuse because they have a physical problem and the tunnel is too small for them to comfortably enter, or an emotional reaction to the tunnel keeps them out. For example, an older arthritic dog who has trouble tucking his head or bending his legs refuses to enter the tunnel for different reasons than a dog who perceives the small space as physically threatening.

TRUST

PREPARATION TIME: 1 minute

LOCATION: Inside

EQUIPMENT: Something unfamiliar for the dog to walk on, another person

Find a small area like a hallway, an entryway, or the entrance to a room and cover it with a substance that is unfamiliar to the dog such as a blue plastic tarp, crumpled newspaper on the floor, large leaf bags, or a grate (make sure the dog's paws cannot slip through and get caught!). Linoleum or tile pieces work great for dogs who have lived only on carpet. The area should be at least three times as wide and as long as the dog.

Stand on one side of the substance while another person holds the dog on the opposite side. Call the dog. If necessary, use food, balls, or toys to encourage the dog to walk over this unfamiliar terrain. Does the dog move freely forward, back up, hesitate and move, or refuse to move?

Circle the best description of the dog's trust.

- Willingly walks on the strange footing
- After a short wait, less than ten seconds, walks on the strange footing
- After a medium wait, between ten and thirty seconds, walks on the strange footing

- Starts to walk on the strange footing, stops, and leaves
- Refuses to walk on the strange footing

Red trots easily over the strange surface. JEFF CANTRELL

IMPLICATIONS FOR TEACHING

Dogs who walk across unusual footing in order to reach you demonstrate how extremely attracted they are to you as well as how much they trust you. Their reliance on you means that schooling sessions can introduce new situations and exercises faster because they willingly follow your directions and guidance.

Dogs who enter, stop, and back out show that although they want to cross it, other fears prevent them.

In real-life situations their performance depends on their location. For example, they sit quietly next to you in the backyard, but at the pet store or the veterinarian's they forget how to sit. Their lack of faith requires schooling sessions that introduce them, in small steps, to new situations only after they are completely comfortable in the current situation. For example, during a two-month period change the location of where the dog is expected to sit quietly to more difficult situations such as inside the house, in the backyard, by a garbage can in the alley, in the front yard, down the block, in the park, and then finally, at the veterinarian's office.

Dogs who refuse to walk on the strange footing may do so for two different reasons. They refuse either because they are not attracted enough to come to you or their fears are so great they must run away or hide. Future schooling sessions must build up a dog's faith in himself and in your relationship.

SOCIABILITY

PREPARATION TIME: 0 minutes
LOCATION: Outside
EQUIPMENT: Another person, hat

Have a person in a hat whom you know, but is unfamiliar to the dog, walk up and talk to you while you stand in the front yard with your dog on-leash. Talk for at least three minutes. Does the dog hide between your legs, go up and sniff the new person, act indifferent or friendly? Does the dog's behavior change after you talk for a while?

If your dog responds well to meeting a stranger, on another day try this: Have someone walk by with a dog and talk with you, or have a person ride past on a bicycle and then come up and talk with you.

Circle the best description of the dog's sociability.

- Bounds up to the new person
- Walks up to the new person
- Waits quietly by your side
- Stays close to you and growls
- Backs away
- Ignores person and wanders off

Do not try this exercise with a dog you think might bite!

IMPLICATIONS FOR TEACHING

Dogs who greet people but do not overpower them with their attention are active, social dogs who are attracted to people. Their friendliness makes them eager to please and they respond quickly to guidance and instructions. For example, teaching "come" is easier because they want to be with you.

Dogs who rush up to people, bouncing and jumping, to greet them are "take-charge" dogs who need effective leadership or they will follow their plans instead of yours. Without lessons to teach them how to listen and focus on you, they can quickly become obnoxious. For example, in teaching "come" they might ignore you if something else captures their attention.

Dogs who wait quietly by your side or back away are somewhat inhibited, but respond excellently to guidance and instructions. For example, teaching "come" requires that you build their enthusiasm and liveliness, so they will want to run to you, rather than walk or wait.

Dogs who ignore other people, wander off, or act indifferent are extremely inhibited, aloof, independent, or mellow. If a dog acts indifferent, compare his performance on this exercise with the other exercises before you design your schooling sessions.

If a dog stays close to you and barks or growls, the dog may be afraid or else he may growl because he is highly territorial. Seek professional assistance.

STRESS

PREPARATION TIME: 5 minutes
LOCATION: Inside
EQUIPMENT: Umbrella, ribbons, strings, cans, small fan

First, you need to create an unusual object. For example, take an umbrella, open it, and tie ribbons and

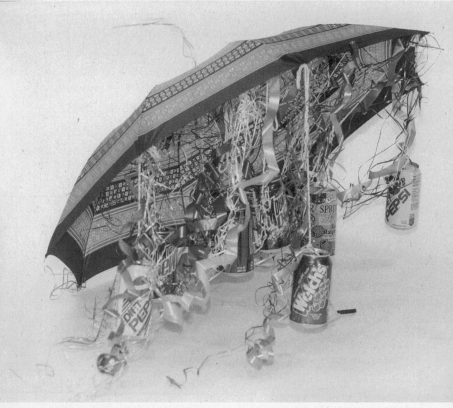

Umbrella close up. LINDA BRUCE

pop cans filled with some pebbles or pennies to its edges, ribs, and top.

When the dog is not with you, place the umbrella on the floor with a small circulating fan blowing on it so that the cans and ribbons move. Now, you are ready for the dog to see it. Call the dog. How does the dog react?

Circle the best description of the dog's stress response.

- Runs up, jumps, paws, or sniffs
- Hesitates and walks around
- Runs or backs away, or hides
- Ignores it

Red investigates the umbrella. LINDA BRUCE

IMPLICATIONS FOR TEACHING

The purpose of this exercise is for you to observe physical symptoms of stress in your dog. That way when your dog displays signs of physical stress you can recognize them without delay and immediately work to reduce your dog's tensions.

To determine dog stress levels look for little indicators such as quivering muscles, clenched and tightened jaws, constricted pupils, tucked, dropped, or tight tails, flat or back ears, panting in short breaths, as well as obvious behaviors such as barking hysterically, destroying shutters or doorjams, whimpering, growling, running away, or hiding.

Dogs under stress indicate it through physical reactions. Highly stressed dogs can remain motionless while their muscles quiver, or they can run around in circles. If your dog does not get stressed by the umbrella's presence, objects may not cause your dog stress. Instead, the dog may be bothered by loud noises, fighting, thunderstorms, or other animals. Learn to recognize your dog's stress response.

Dogs who are stressed cannot learn or perform effectively. If your dog stresses easily, before you work with him you must reduce the amount of stress he carries in his body. One of the best ways to relieve dogs' emotional, mental, and physical stress is to give them a five-minute Animal Energetics session at least once every day, or three times a day for highly stressed dogs. Practicing Animal Energetics establishes a relaxation response. Then you can teach and the dog can listen to you and learn.

Handler-Dog Interaction Exercises

ATTRACTION TO HANDLER—EXERCISE 1

PREPARATION TIME: 0 minutes
LOCATION: Inside
EQUIPMENT: No equipment needed

When you come home from work or running errands, immediately watch television, read a magazine, newspaper, or book, or do something to occupy yourself for fifteen minutes. Do not pay any attention to the dog. How many different techniques does the dog use to get your attention? How long does it take before the dog gives up?

Circle the best description of the dog's interest in you.

- Barks to get your attention
- Nuzzles you with his nose
- Brings you a toy or ball
- Lays down at your feet so he can touch you
- Finds a place in the same room, rests quietly, or chews on a bone or toy
- Leaves and goes to a different room
- Ignores you

ATTRACTION TO HANDLER—EXERCISE 2

PREPARATION TIME: 1 minute
LOCATION: Inside
EQUIPMENT: Treat, toy, ball

After an all-day absence place a food treat, a toy, and a ball in the middle of the room. Then, sit on a chair in the same room. Is the dog attracted to one of the items or does he want your attention?

Circle the best description of the dog's interest in you.

- Immediately plays with toy or eats treat
- Brings you the toy or ball to play with him
- Ignores the items and wants to be with you

IMPLICATIONS FOR TEACHING

These two exercises indicate the amount of attraction you hold for your dog. Social attraction is a significant factor because the effectiveness of your teaching program hinges on the type of relationship you have with your dog. Dogs who want to be with their handlers learn faster and easier.

The second exercise allows you to determine your placement in a dog's priorities. There is nothing wrong if a dog focuses his attention on the toy or ball, eats the food, and ignores you. Instead, it helps you design appropriate schooling sessions.

EFFECT OF HANDLER ATTITUDE—EXERCISE 1

PREPARATION TIME: 0 minutes
LOCATION: Inside
EQUIPMENT: No equipment needed

Ask the dog to join you in a room. Close the door. Sit on the floor. Do not talk, move, or gesture but think angry and unhappy thoughts for the first minute. Then, add words, sounds, and body language to your feelings. However, do not direct them at the dog. During the next thirty seconds use a deeper, lower voice and let the inflection drop at the end of your phrases. Feel the emotion pouring out. Does the dog come up to you, avoid you, get nervous, or ignore you?

Now, change and think happy and excited thoughts for one minute. Then, add words, sounds, and body language to your feelings. During the next thirty seconds use a happy voice with a higher pitch. Let the inflection rise at the end of your phrases. Feel the emotion pouring out. Does the dog's reaction change?

Circle the best description of the dog's reaction to your negative attitude. Does the dog react more when you add words, feelings, and body language?

- Comes up to you
- Avoids you
- Acts nervous
- Backs away
- Ignores you

Circle the best description of the dog's reaction to your positive attitude. Does the dog react more when you add words, feelings, and body language?

- Comes up to you
- Avoids you
- Acts nervous
- Backs away
- Ignores you

EFFECT OF HANDLER ATTITUDE—EXERCISE 2

PREPARATION TIME: 0 minutes
LOCATION: Inside
EQUIPMENT: Another person

With a person the dog knows and likes stage a loud, noisy, yelling, screaming, nonphysical "fight" for one to two minutes. How does the dog react? If you cannot find another person, pretend to have a fight while you talk on the phone.

Circle the best description of the dog's reaction to stress.

- Comes up, circles, sniffs, barks
- Comes up, growls, and lunges
- Watches and waits quietly
- Watches and shakes, trembles, averts eyes
- Cowers under something
- Leaves and hides in another room

IMPLICATIONS FOR TEACHING

These two exercises show the effect that your attitude and voice have on your dog. Dogs not only see obvious signals such as a hand signal to indicate down, but they also read your hidden feelings. The voice you use can radically change a dog's performance. For example, no one, person or dog, wants to come to an angry person who yells in a loud, threatening voice "COME!" Yet most dogs are eager to run up to someone who is happy and uses a light bubbly voice saying "Commmme!"

When you are stressed or upset due to a bad day at work, a fight with a neighbor or son, or an accident where you trip and hit your shin against the table, your dog feels it. Dogs absorb tension. Before you start a schooling session or leave the house, make sure your dog is not impacted negatively by your attitude. Otherwise, your dog's ability to learn will be affected, and the dog may chew, bark, defecate, or try countless other undesirable behaviors to relieve his pent-up tensions when you leave home. Use Animal Energetics sessions to relieve a dog's mental, emotional, and physical stress. When dogs are faced with situations they cannot control or understand, they need your help.

Part 2

THE SECRET:
Catch Your Dog Doing
Something Right

CHAPTER 4

SEVEN QUALITIES OF SUCCESSFUL DOG HANDLERS

Working with dogs is like planting a garden. You want to eat fresh carrots, tomatoes, and green peppers, but first you have to plant the seeds. In the beginning, you accidentally mix all the seeds together. Now, you cannot tell marigold seeds from cucumber seeds. You think you are planting daisies, and onions grow. You put tomato plants in the bright sun, and they wilt. You overwater the tomatoes, and they rot. Finally, you realize that growing a garden requires you to figure out what each plant needs. You learn about watering, mulching, spraying, and sunlight.

Dogs, like plants, grow the way they are cultivated. Certain handler characteristics such as acting enthusiastically, teaching not training, eliminating judging and negative thinking, insisting that the relationship comes first, believing mistakes do not mean failure, using five-minute schooling sessions, and catching a dog doing something right can harvest a cornucopia of good behaviors.

The First Quality: Act Enthusiastically

Sara was five feet five, slender, and her long blond hair trailed down her back in a tightly woven braid. Her shoulders bent forward as she gripped the leash with both hands, dug her heels into the ground, and pulled the giant schnauzer along. Thin bright red lips popped from a pale face. Tiny grunts and small curses interrupted the silence. With each step the dog lagged further behind until the leash stretched out behind the woman like a riverboat's towline. After five more steps, Sara stopped and yelled, "I had a miserable day and now this. Take him away from me!" Sara's twelve-year-old son ran up to the dog, grabbed his leash, and the schnauzer pulled the boy as they raced out the door. In one instant the schnauzer changed from barge to speedboat.

When I asked Sara in an earlier telephone conversation if she believed enthusiasm was an important quality when working with a dog, she responded, "Of course." Yet in class Sara said, "I cannot be enthusiastic, I feel hostile. I've had a hard day at work. I work my dog in the dark every night, and my car had two flat

tires this week. I can't generate enthusiasm for myself.
How can I generate it for my dog?"

Lack of enthusiasm kills any teaching efforts and
stops a dog's learning. Attitude is a chain that ties your
dog's performance to you with either cast-iron bonds,
rubber bands, or silken threads.

Before you work with your dog, check your mind-
set. If you feel tired, dull, crabby, or hostile, adjust your
attitude. Take ten minutes and read a magazine article,
listen to a favorite song, watch part of a football follies
tape, or talk to a friend; the possibilities are limitless.
Once you feel your exhaustion and staleness slip away,
call your dog and begin the schooling session.

An enthusiastic attitude animates dogs and keeps
them eager to learn. You do not have to whoop and
holler or constantly bounce up and down to work with
your dog. Dogs respond to smiles, grins, laughter, and
cheerfulness. You can also clap your hands, whistle,
skip, or leap with joy. Just remember, good behavior
starts with you. When a dog is right, reward him with
enthusiasm.

The Second Quality: Teach, Do Not Train

When I was in kindergarten, my friend Connie
wanted to be a teacher. It took me much longer. I did
not choose teaching as my career until my junior year
at the university. For two years I absorbed books, work-
shops, and experiences that could tell me about teaching. At first, I believed teaching occurred inside
classrooms. Later, I learned that teaching happens all

the time. Dogs also can participate in the excitement of learning.

Dogs are wonderful students: willing, creative, lively, and responsive. The challenge for teachers is to recognize what a dog knows, build on that knowledge, and encourage the dog's ability to learn. When dogs are recognized as intelligent, active learners and not treated as servants, robots, or dumb animals, they respond by learning quickly and easily.

Teaching time is not restricted to official work sessions. Teaching happens throughout the day. Every interaction you have with dogs is a learning opportunity. If you encourage Muffy the puppy to jump on you when you come home from work, she will also jump to greet you, your friends, and other family members when Muffy grows into a fifty-five-pound dalmatian. Instead, you can teach Muffy to sit *before* you touch her and refuse to recognize or touch her until she sits or stands quietly. Then, Muffy learns that the amount and type of attention she receives depends on her actions. Muffy eventually realizes that if she sits, stands, or lies down when you enter the house, she receives your complete attention. By the time Muffy grows into an adult dog, you have completely avoided any jumping problem.

A training approach concentrates on the physical aspects of working with dogs. Varying amounts of force are used to control dogs, from special collars and training devices to domination techniques such as requiring dogs to perform submissive downs so that the handlers can demonstrate their position as pack leader.

A physical training approach emphasizes a dog's instinctual responses to authority and force. Trainers who use it believe they control a dog's actions. As a result, these techniques work only with a dog's body and not his mind. In the case of Muffy, the jumping puppy, a physical-training approach might use a knee in the chest, a push to shove her off balance, or a collar jerk to pull her away. This physical approach may stop Muffy's jumping, but it does not teach Muffy what behavior is acceptable instead of jumping.

Teachers recognize that dogs think, process information, and learn. They want to expand a dog's thinking ability. Their goal is to figure out how individual dogs learn so they can teach dogs to comprehend different situations.

Teachers know that dogs make choices and believe that dogs control their own behavior. Teachers instruct dogs and create learning experiences to develop a dog's mind so it can control the dog's instinctual responses. Teachers believe that once a dog's mind engages, his body follows.

Teachers encourage dogs to use their minds because they know someday a dog will encounter a situation where his instincts will want to take over. If they train just the dog's body, when his instincts surface, the dog will respond to his inner drives. However, if they teach him to think, the dog will listen to them for information and guidance in spite of his instincts.

Jesse James, a six-month-old border collie, demonstrated how working with a dog's mind—building up his confidence and trust—can change a timid, overly sensitive dog to a friendly companion.

Jesse James seemed to house two different dog personalities in his body. At times, Jesse could be independent, ready to nip at Steve's or Donna's heels (his human parents), or herd them into the kitchen or hallway. However, during walks Jesse crawled between their legs, clinging to them when other animals, cars, or even trees appeared. When Steve acted "tough" with Jesse, he got worse. By the time Jesse was six months old, Steve and Donna realized that Jesse was afraid of his own shadow, but he also ignored them when his independent side surfaced.

At our first meeting, when I heard Steve drive up to my office, I walked out to his car to greet them. Jesse immediately jumped over the backseat and cowered by the rear window. I waited quietly and did not reach for Jesse, but stayed inside the car with my hand stretched out. Finally, Jesse's border collie curiosity could not be contained. He sniffed my hand and shyly followed us to my office. As I talked with Steve, Jesse was encouraged to roam the office and get acquainted with it on his terms, not our terms.

Once Steve understood that today's lesson focused on developing his understanding and listening skills, Steve started watching Jesse closely. Steve learned that Jesse viewed cars, bicycles, and other animals as threats to his survival. Developing Jesse's confidence required a change in Steve's behavior so that Steve would not be perceived as a threat. Each lesson increased Jesse's confidence. He learned he could listen to Steve and Donna and depend on their input no matter where he was or what happened. Four sessions later, Jesse's timidity disappeared. Now, he pulls his fellow border collie, Sara Sue, in a cart in the park unafraid of noises, other animals, and his shadow.

The Third Quality: Eliminate Judging and Negative Thinking

Sally's gentle voice pleaded with me on the phone. "Please help my poodle. I know it's not her fault. She vomits every time we take her in the Land Rover. I'll do whatever it takes." As we talked, I contrasted Sally's demeanor with her daughter Karen's message: "Call me right away. The dog is neurotic. She has to stop this or I will take her to the pound."

People constantly make judgments about their dog's behavior, describing it as good, bad, neurotic, hyperactive, and other subjective characteristics. Yet emotional opinions obscure a handler's ability to determine the reasons behind a dog's actions. Avoid destroying work sessions by thinking negative thoughts such as, "I know the dog will be bad," or "The dog is so dumb, he will never learn."

Instead, evaluate a dog's behavior without making any judgments. Replace words such as stupid, crazy, bully, or wimp with factual behavior assessments. For example, "Bart chases his tail and circles for one to five minutes when my two- and four-year-old children run through the house chasing each other, or if he hears sirens, cars backfire, or loud voices."

Detailed behavioral observations can help you uncover the hidden reasons behind a dog's behavior. When you start watching, you can see what was previously hidden. Then, you can understand that the children's activity causes Bart to get so excited that he runs in circles to get rid of his excess energy. When you realize that the problem is not Bart circling but how to direct Bart's excess energy, you can effectively address the situation. Now, when the children run and play, you can channel Bart's energy by having him chase a ball, bringing him inside so their play does not disturb his equilibrium, or practicing Animal Energetics. When you understand that Bart is sound sensitive, you can play soft music throughout the house to mask outside noises. Also, you can lower voices or shut doors and windows so that loud noises do not disturb him. By investigating instead of judging, you can see beyond symptoms and into root causes.

Your new role as detective rather than judge allows you to evaluate the actions of a dog based on objective criteria. Then, during a simple conversation on the telephone, you, too, can determine that the poodle vomits in the Land Rover only in the summer because the back windows cannot open and the lack of fresh air makes her sick.

The Fourth Quality: Insist That the Relationship Come First

On the phone the man asked me to meet his service dog Dexter and determine if Dexter was still happy helping him. At two o'clock on Saturday afternoon, the man wheeled into my office as Dexter, his three-legged, seven-year-old service dog hopped next to his chair.

During the ensuing conversation, I learned that Dexter had lost his leg to bone cancer three years earlier. Now, the man was concerned that Dexter moved with more difficulty and wondered if Dexter should be retired. If Dexter retired, the man would face many additional challenges in his daily chores, since other service dogs were not currently available. During the entire conversation the man did not complain about Dexter; his only concern was for Dexter's comfort. He explained that Dexter had helped him, and now it was his turn to help Dexter.

As I watched, the rapport between the two of them was obvious. Dexter acted before he was asked. The man was attentive to Dexter's needs. He wanted what was best for Dexter and not just best for him. I could tell from their intuitive responses to each other that I was in the presence of a gift: a friendship where each partner freely gives what the other one requires.

Relationships are like current arcing between two poles. The energy surges, resists, or explodes on impact, but an electrical charge always flows. Dogs and handlers also generate an invisible energy that can move smoothly or burn on contact. This relationship between dog and handler defines every contact from dinnertime manners to playtime roles. It is the invisible current that transforms ordinary associations into extraordinary friendships.

Your relationship affects your dog's performance. However, relationships consist of more than a short response time to signals and instant obedience. Relationships are recognized by the rapport between you and your dog. They are characterized by your awareness that each of you can have different agendas. You want to walk quietly through the forest, but your beagle runs off to chase rodents and rabbits. Now, you must find a mutually agreeable compromise to resolve your differences. It is not that your dog is more important than you, or you are more important than your dog, but *we* come first.

Extraordinary friendships eliminate the "I" and replace it with "we." Each partner balances the needs of the other against his desires. Your dog does what you ask because you have learned how to combine what your dog needs with what you want. When you accept this responsibility, three-legged service dogs do not retire at age seven but willingly work for three more years because when "we" come first, "I" can always perform.

The Fifth Quality: Believe Mistakes Do Not Mean Failure

It was a perfect down-stay. Red was quiet and unmoving, so I opened the door and walked outside. When I walked back in the door, I glanced at him. Fifteen feet away he was still lying quietly. Without a pause, I dropped on my knees and hopped in a circle. Red looked my way but held his position. Then I stood up and walked three feet to the wall in front of me, faced it, and practiced leg lifts against the wall for thirty seconds. Next, I walked directly in front of him and turned my back. I walked ten feet away, turned around and faced him. Red was curious, but still had not moved. Then, I pushed it. I dropped to my knees and looked at him. Instantly, he got up and walked toward me. I walked him back and placed him in the down-stay position again. I walked ten feet away, faced Red, and dropped to my knees. Again, he broke. Again, I returned him to his spot and asked him to down-stay. This time as I walked to a spot six feet in front of him, I realized that Red was already following me. I stopped and brought him back to his down-stay spot. At that moment the judge at the practice dog show called, "Return to your dogs."

On our ride home I reviewed what happened. Thoughts fast as greyhounds raced through my mind: "I should have known he'd break, I should have stopped earlier, I should have noticed his ears were starting to fold back, I really blew it." Luckily, after fifteen minutes of self-deprecating comments, I stopped and realized that Red and I had stumbled but we did not fall down the cliff and break our legs. Red and I had more to learn. Mistakes happen when dogs learn something different, a handler tries new techniques, or hidden problems surface.

Successful people make mistakes. Great dogs make mistakes. Mistakes are early-warning signals that flag our attention when dogs do not understand what we want.

Learning takes time. So what if a dog goofs? Will the world grind to a halt? Will the dog never be able to learn? Dogs learn continually. When we accept that mistakes happen because perfect dogs and people do not exist, we can give ourselves and our dogs permission to go up like a rocket and down like a stick.

Faults, miscalculations, or blunders are not the issue. Instead, it's how we act after a mistake occurs; we can either focus on the problem or we can concentrate on the solution. Dwelling on errors magnifies them and turns them into roadblocks. Instead, we need to uncover their causes. Four ideas can speed you in this recovery process.

1. ASK QUESTIONS

Analyze the situation. Think about what went wrong and employ questions to determine what actually happened. Ask questions such as, what caused Red to break in the down-stay? Did I lose my concentration, focus, or quiet? Was the type of distraction inappropriate for his level of training? Was he tired at the end of the session? Did I ask him too early for a behavior? Questions are a valuable teaching tool because every problem contains its own solution, if we can only access it.

2. ACCEPT EQUAL RESPONSIBILITY FOR ANY MISTAKE

You and your dog are members of the same team. His learning depends on your teaching ability. Your teaching depends on his physical, mental, and emotional aptitude. He is bread dough and you are the baker; he rises to your instructions.

3. DO NOT CONFUSE MISTAKES WITH FAILURE

Failure is an opinion, not a fact. It exists only if you quit trying and accept the situation.

4. GROW A RESPONSE

In the same way an eleven-month-old infant re-quires the support of loving hands as she takes her first steps, nurture your dog's first efforts. Just like mothers who know eleven-month-old infants cannot participate in 10K runs, realize your dog passes through many learning stages before he can give consistent, polished performances.

When you look for new answers, you find them. Un-limited solutions exist. Your dog does not have to go up like a rocket and down like a stick, but can float in the sky like a hot air balloon supported by your under-standing.

The Sixth Quality:
Use Five-Minute Schooling Sessions

0:05 Five minutes is a long time when the entire lesson is focused and concentrates on bring-ing the best out of you and your dog. Experi-ment. Set your oven timer for five minutes and just sit there, doing nothing, waiting. How many seconds or minutes go by before you look at the clock for the first time or the third time? Imagine eating a bowl of ice cream for five minutes, or pretend that you are sitting in the dentist's chair for five minutes while he drills your tooth. Both take five minutes, but which do you prefer? The content of your five-minute schooling ses-sions can be either fun for your dog or stressful. Plan them carefully and your dog will learn quickly, happily, and eagerly.

Five-minute sessions have three major advantages for you and your dog. First, you can conduct at least one practice session every day. Consistency creates responsive and reliable dog behavior. Second, you can focus the content on just one idea or behavior. Short sessions prevent dogs from becoming overwhelmed with too much information and too many directions. Third, your dog learns that schooling is fun because short, stimulating lessons maintain the dog's excitement.

In five minutes you can teach dogs the mechanics of most behaviors, such as sit or down, and associate the physical action with a specific word signal. If you divide five minutes into ten-second schooling sessions, you have thirty sessions. Imagine how fast your dog could learn to sit if you had thirty mini-schooling sessions every day. For example, at 7:00 A.M. as Rex walks into the bathroom while you brush your teeth, you introduce "sit" for the first time with a food lure. Three more ten-second sessions and it's shower time. After you shower, four ten-second sit sessions. In the kitchen before Rex eats his breakfast meal, you ask him to sit. Eureka! He gets a huge reward for that sit—breakfast. Later on, when he nudges you with his nose for a little scratching, you ask him for another sit. By 8:30 A.M. Rex has already had ten ten-second practice sessions before you leave for the day. In the evening, you can use your remaining three and a half minutes of practice time to work on sit again, introduce down, teach a trick, or start solving a behavior problem. If your schedule permits, you can plan more than one five-minute session during the day. When teaching takes just five minutes, there is always time for schooling your dog.

The Seventh Quality:
Catch a Dog Doing Something Right

The five foot, four inch woman was dragged into my office by an eleven-inch Jack Russell terrier. As we talked, she pulled the padded blue metal chair closer to me, thinking, I suppose, that if she decreased the physical proximity between us, her improved hearing ability would increase her understanding. But her eyes glazed over as I repeated, "Find ninety-five reasons to praise your dog every day."

Her dog had already bitten her daughter's hand and bitten her arm. She came to my office to complain about her dog's behavior. She expected me to agree that he was a bad dog and to give her a magic wand to wave over the dog's head so that in one instant the eighteen-month-old dog would quit biting and not be hyperactive. Unfortunately for her, magic wands do not exist. Luckily, however, we can use words, deeds, and feelings to create our own magic. We just need to catch a dog doing something right.

The woman's wide eyes blinked furiously when I said that saying "no, no, no" all day long would not cause the biting or the hyperactivity to disappear. Instead, I said, by concentrating on the dog's misdeeds, her constant corrections increased the number and strength of the mistakes. Her body sunk deeper into the chair when I explained that her constant reprimands no longer meant anything to her dog. His behavior had become worse because he had tuned her out.

Dogs cannot learn correct behavior from hearing the word "no." Saying "no" tells dogs not to do something, but it does not teach dogs what behavior is preferred. If you say "Yes, this is what I want. Good boy!" a dog recognizes the specific action he performed that earned a positive response.

Your goal as your dog's handler is to find reasons for a dog to receive praise, food rewards, and positive attention. For example, "Oh, look, Greta is sitting quietly. Good girl. Oh, you are watching me, good girl. What a lovely down, good girl. That was a nice deep breath, good girl. Good watch at the door, looking at the kitty with no barking, good girl." Find reasons outside of your official training sessions to praise your dog. In a short amount of time, you will discover that your dog's behavior improves.

During the one-hour session with the Jack Russell, he never bit, growled, or chased. Within fifteen minutes he sat for a few seconds, then stood, then sat again. Finally, he laid down and rested his head on the floor. His hyperactivity disappeared without one "no." All I did was praise him for being good whenever he offered a quiet behavior.

When you catch a dog doing something right, he learns without effort or stress.

CHAPTER 5

playSMART:

Happy Dogs Learn Faster

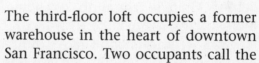 The third-floor loft occupies a former warehouse in the heart of downtown San Francisco. Two occupants call the loft home: a single woman, Lynn, and her sixty-five-pound golden retriever, Grace. It is a typical day, and they are doing what suits them best, playing ball on top of the four-story building.

Lynn threw out all the rules that said dogs cannot live happily in one of the largest metropolitan cities in the United States. Instead, Lynn uses rooftops, city streets, beaches, and parks to give Grace the exercise, fun, and attention that happy dogs require daily.

However, Lynn sought my assistance when Grace stopped one block before home and refused to move for ten, twenty, or thirty minutes. Grace's weight was a large fraction of Lynn's, so dragging her home was not an option. Instead, Lynn coaxed and pleaded until eventually Grace moved.

I explained to Lynn that we needed to understand the thinking that caused Grace to "put on the brakes." First, we looked at their walk, but Lynn had not changed their route and still walked Grace for one hour. Next, we analyzed where Grace stopped, but there were no new shops, strangers, or scary objects in that location. Then, we looked at how much time they spent together and we discovered what changed: Lynn now traveled frequently out of state and left Grace with friends and neighbors. Even when Lynn was home she had less time to spend with Grace. Grace had learned that after a walk, Lynn left for the day or a week. Finally, we had uncovered the reason behind Grace's refusal to go home. Grace wanted more attention and time with Lynn.

Once we understood Grace's thinking, dealing with her stopping was simple. Our task was to turn the trip back to the loft into a game. In most situations, two magic words, "Let's play!" can break routines, turn bad situations into good ones, and change slow learners into fast learners. We enlisted Lynn's neighbor to help us, and we played turning for home into a game of chase. On other walks we brought Grace's ball and played fetch. Lynn fit more time with Grace into her schedule, and once again Grace entered the loft easily.

Dogs need to have fun. Attempting to drag Grace home would only have increased her resistance. Yet, it is almost impossible for any dog to resist chasing balls, food rewards, and people who are laughing, bright, and bubbly. Dogs learn faster when schooling sessions feel like playtime.

A play format uses dogs' natural enthusiasm and energy to help them learn. It reduces the tension dogs experience in artificial situations where they are pushed or forced to sit or down. Instead, food lures, toys, happy voices, bouncing balls, active feet, and games motivate dogs to offer desired behaviors.

To understand why happy dogs learn faster, think about how listening to a bluegrass fiddler makes you feel. At the first touch of his bow to the strings your heart starts beating faster. Barely a minute passes by and your hands hit your legs keeping time to the beat. The fiddler hits a crescendo and your feet start bouncing and your hands start clapping. Before long your whole body wants to join in and the next thing you know you are up and dancing.

Dogs, like people, dance. They also walk, run, jump, leap, crawl, roll over, and bow. To discover what a dog thinks watch how he moves. Dance with your dog to solve problems, teach him new behaviors, or build a better relationship.

Jettison old training ideas such as commanding the dog to obey, pushing the dog into position, or forcing the dog to listen. Instead, replace them with a play-SMART approach that uses toys, games, exercise, and adventures to motivate dogs, strengthen dog bodies, stimulate dog minds, and create happy hearts.

Dogs need exercise. Playing ball with a dog is not a replacement for the sustained cardiovascular exercise that comes with a walk. Walking oxygenates the entire body; hearts beat stronger, muscles get firmer, lungs expand, and that's just the beginning! Dogs who walk on a regular basis are in better physical condition, which means they can live longer with fewer health problems.

Besides creating healthy bodies, walking builds healthy minds. Dogs who never leave home can become more timid, anxious, or assertive when people visit, the meter reader comes, or children play or ride their bikes in front of the house. Yet, if dogs are accustomed to seeing different people, animals, and objects on their walks, they can face new experiences without barking, submissively urinating, or hiding in the closet.

Walks can be as short as five minutes or as long as one hour. Find the amount of time that fits comfortably with your schedule. Ten-minute walks every day are more valuable than a one-hour walk once a month.

Ideally, you should walk your dog every day. Realistically, try to find the time to walk your dog three times a week. Practically, you can walk your dog at least once during a weekend. Dogs love to feel the grass under their paws, pick up scents from low-lying bushes, and spend time with their handler. If you can only do one thing with your dog every day, take him on a walk.

Look at it from a dog's point of view. What part of your anatomy does he see most? Your feet. Like a telegraph, use your feet to tap messages: listen to me, come to me, watch me, play with me.

To get a dog's attention move like a dancer, not like a soldier. Put a bounce in your step that says watch me, I'm having fun. Vary your speed, walk fast, walk slow, run four steps. Stop. Turn around. Skip right for twenty feet. Drop to your knees and keep moving. Jump up and down in place. Laugh. Do the unexpected. Use your steps to capture your dog's attention.

I use two types of walks in my teaching program. "Walkies" allow the dog to sniff and explore as long as he keeps within five or six feet of me and does not pull on the leash. "Work-time" walks require the dog at specific intervals to sit, down, stay, stand, fetch, or perform whatever behavior we happen to be working on at the moment. After the dog offers the behavior, his reward, besides the occasional food reward, is that the walk continues. For example, walk ten steps and ask the dog to sit. Walk twenty steps and ask the dog to down. Walk five steps and ask the dog to stand-stay. Walk forty steps and ask the dog to fetch. Walk ten steps and ask the dog to sit. Run ten steps. Ask the dog to down. Walk slowly for fourteen steps. Walk normally for fifty steps.

Work-time walks solve dog behavior problems with a minimal amount of effort because they focus a dog's mind, direct his attention to you, and stimulate his ability to think of the correct response. In the same way you get physically tired from figuring out your income tax returns or working at a desk job, dogs also become physically tired from "brain work." Since many behavior problems are caused by overactive dogs, you can use work-time walks to relax your dog's mind, body, and behavior.

However, walks are just one tool in a teacher's toolbox. Dogs love games too. Games build on each dog's natural abilities to hunt, track, fetch, or burrow. They build on a dog's talents and interests, promote learning, and develop the dog's trust and confidence. Best of all, games teach dogs that learning is fun.

Five simple rules ensure that your playSMART sessions will experience success:

1. Play with a dog before, not after, he eats.
2. Find a location that has few distractions.
3. Plan your playtime so it does not interfere with a regularly scheduled event; for example, your daughter arriving home from school in the afternoon.
4. Play games that are appropriate for your dog's age, weight, health, or physical condition.
5. Play your favorite music and use its tempo to animate your feet. Play children's songs, marches, top 40, oldies, or show tunes to keep your steps lively and your mood upbeat.

Try the following five games.

GAME 1: POP GOES THE WEASEL

PURPOSE: To teach dogs to pay attention and focus.

Find the children's song "Pop Goes the Weasel." If you cannot find that song, choose one that has a specific refrain that occurs throughout the song at short intervals. Put the song on and call your dog's name while he sits in front of you.

Say "look at me," "attention," or any words that mean watch me. Get his attention by waving a ball, wiggling a food treat, or squeaking a toy. Place the food treat between your lips, or put the ball or toy under your chin. As soon as you hear the words "Pop goes the weasel," let the food treat "pop" from your mouth, or raise your chin and let the ball drop down to the dog.

At first the dog may not understand. However, in a short time the dog will learn the game requires watching you, and when he does, he earns rewards. Keep the dog's attention by changing locations.

GAME 2: SEVENTY-SIX TROMBONES

PURPOSE: To teach dogs to sit.

Find the song "Seventy-six Trombones." If you cannot find that song, select a song or a march with a pounding beat. Put the song on and start marching. Call your dog's name. Say "sit." Use food, toys, or balls to lure him into the sit if he cannot sit when asked. (Turn to pages 118–124 to learn how to teach sit with a lure.) Ask the dog to sit at different locations while you march for the length of the song.

GAME 3: LULLABY

PURPOSE: To prevent dogs from jumping on people or running through doors by teaching down-stay.

Find a song that is quiet and calm. For example, "When the Lion Sleeps Tonight" from the *Lion King* movie, or "Pachelbel's Canon," or soft crooner music. Play the song. Walk to the front door and ask your dog to down. Use food, toys, or balls to lure him into the down if he cannot lay down when asked. (Turn to pages 124–130 to learn how to teach down with a lure.)

Lie down next to the dog for at least fifteen seconds. Next, stand next to the dog while he lies down. Once he stays quietly, ask someone to open and close the door while you lie next to him. (To prevent a dog from escaping out an open door attach his leash and hold it in your hand.) Try "sleeping" at the back door, a bedroom door, or any other door. If you are outside ask the dog to lay down by different trees or bushes.

GAME 4: COME A LITTLE BIT CLOSER—PART 1

PURPOSE: To teach dogs to come.

My favorite song for this is "Come a Little Bit Closer" by Jay & the Americans. Just hearing the music gets my feet tapping. Play this song or any song that has a driving beat. Now, fasten the leash to your dog and run backwards while you call the dog's name. Feel free to laugh, giggle, and clap your hands. When the dog reaches you, praise and reward him. Repeat.

If you are in an enclosed yard, take the dog off-leash and play this chase game.

COME A LITTLE BIT CLOSER—PART 2

Turn off the song and build a jump by securing cardboard across a doorway or fastening a fishing rod on top of two stacks of books at least three feet apart. The height of the jump should not be higher than the highest point on the dog's back. If you are outside, attach a pole on top of two cement blocks at least three feet apart. Walk up to the jump with your dog and step over it together.

Turn on the music. Ask someone to hold your dog until you walk over the jump and call him. Stand at

least three feet away from the jump. Tap the jump with
your hand. Back away until you are at least three feet
from the jump. Then, bounce up and down, clap your
hands, and wiggle a favorite treat, toy, or ball. Wave it
so the dog sees it. Say, "Duchess come!" Praise and reward the dog when she comes to you. Repeat a few
times.

If you have space in your yard, add a second jump.
Then, build three or four jumps in a row.

 Do not jump dogs who are under a year old.

GAME 5: FOLLOW THE LEADER

PURPOSE: To teach dogs to walk and focus.

Draw a squiggly design on the floor of your garage,
driveway, or backyard that is at least ten feet wide and
has lots of loops. You can use chalk or masking tape on
cement or tar, sticks or screwdrivers on dirt, and spray
chalk or anything that leaves an impression on grass.

Hold the dog's leash with your left hand. With your
right hand, hold a tablespoon. Place a tennis ball, toy,
or treat on it so that the dog easily sees it. Without looking at the spoon, follow the design you have drawn.
At every intersection of two lines, ask the dog to sit or
down.

If the item falls off while you walk, great. Let your dog get it. Then, replace the ball or add a new treat on your spoon and keep walking. Once you can walk the design, try running or skipping it. If your dog likes Frisbees, place a Frisbee on your head and follow the design.

The number of games you can play with your dog are limitless. You can ask dogs to crawl under tables to find toys, go through your arms to earn treats, tunnel under chairs covered by sheets—anything is possible. Let your imagination run wild.

Just remember, dance with your dog. The play-SMART approach develops dogs who are mentally alert and focused, physically able, confident, and happy. Your responsibility is to create play situations that teach.

CHAPTER **6**

REMOVING THE MYSTERY FROM DOG TRAINING

Jim stands quietly in the middle of the living room and shouts, "Trek, front door." A black chow runs down the staircase, sails across the tiled entryway, and waits expectantly in a sit by the front door. Jim walks over to the hallway closet, pulls out Trek's leash, and they head for a walk. The next day Jim stands quietly in the middle of the living room and shouts, "Trek, garage door." Trek careens around the kitchen corner, leaps over a small floor cushion, and waits expectantly in a sit by the door that leads to the garage. Jim walks over to the door, opens it, and Jim and Trek enter the garage ready for a car ride to the Dairy Queen. At least four times every day Jim stands in his living room, shouts, "Trek, back door," and watches Trek fly through the air jumping over stools, leaping over newspapers and magazines piled in little heaps by the couch, ottoman, and barstool, to land by the door that allows the dog to go outside to do his business.

Dogs choose between alternatives constantly. When handlers, like Jim, encourage dogs to make decisions, dogs learn that the correct choice earns rewards. Trek recognizes three separate signals, "front door," "back door," "garage door," and the corresponding action on his part that each signal requires.

Before you begin working with your dog, evaluate your verbal and nonverbal communication skills. For example, affection can be conveyed through smiling, friendly rubs, or a loving feeling, and not just through words such as "good dog" or food treats. People "talk" all the time to their dogs without using words. Take a few minutes and think about the unconscious gestures, facial expressions, body language, or feelings that are present in your daily interactions with your dog. If you are not sure of your reactions, ask someone to film you and your dog while you play and then teach a lesson. Then, you can identify the messages you send. For example, Maxine wants her dog, Dusty, not to beg at the kitchen table. Yet while Maxine says "Go to your place," her hand drops down and scratches Dusty on the head. Result: Dusty stays by her side at the kitchen table.

How you communicate with a dog affects his ability to listen, the length of time it takes him to learn new exercises, his stress level, and his attitude. Your challenge is to use verbal and nonverbal signals effectively.

If your speech delivery is clear and distinct, your dog has a better chance of physically hearing your words. Use your tone of voice to affect the dog's ability to focus on you and pay attention. For example, a higher pitch with a rising inflection at the end of a word, phrase, or sentence indicates pleasure, fun, and happiness. A lower pitch with a dropping inflection at the end indicates seriousness and disapproval.

Avoid speaking in a monotone. The pitch of your voice should vary in order to attract or maintain a dog's attention. However, if your volume increases only when a dog misbehaves, you can scream, but a dog can still ignore you.

Dogs can hear sounds people cannot. You can whisper and a dog can hear it. If a dog ignores your signal, do not yell louder at the dog. The dog can physically hear you. The problem is not your voice's volume; the issue is that the dog has not learned to pay attention to you.

Nonverbal signals telegraph your thoughts and feelings to dogs by movements as quick as an eyeblink, a nod of the head, a flash of a smile, or the appearance of a frown. Dogs read facial expressions constantly. A serious expression can be interpreted as disapproval if you grimace, purse your lips, raise one eyebrow, or wrinkle your forehead.

Your body language emphasizes your words. Hands clenched into fists, arms held tightly next to sides, or angry gestures shout displeasure. In contrast, a relaxed body posture, nodding your head in approval, skipping steps, and quiet or expressive hands send a welcoming message.

Even your breathing makes a difference. When you are nervous, tense, or upset, your breathing becomes shallow, jagged, or uneven. Frequently, when people concentrate they hold their breath. How you breathe reflects your state of mind, and dogs are very sensitive to what their handlers are thinking and feeling. When I want a nervous dog to relax, I make a point of breathing deeply and slowly from my diaphragm. I consciously relax my hands to prevent sending any additional stress to the dog through his leash. I smile, nod my head, and use soft and happy tones to encourage him. I do not stare into the dog's eyes. Instead, I watch his body.

The amount of physical contact you have with a dog usually corresponds to the amount of physical contact you desire. For example, one of my clients is an elderly woman who constantly touches her Pekingese. When she makes dinner, the dog is in the kitchen at her feet. While she watches television, the dog sits with her on the couch. When she goes to bed at night the dog sleeps with her. For them, they have the perfect relationship. Yet I have another client who allows her Pekingese only in the kitchen and the backyard, even when someone is at home. She touches the dog occasionally, but spends most of her time away from him. Her dog accepts this way of life and displays no problem behaviors.

Each client developed a relationship that suited her lifestyle. Acceptable behavior depends on the viewer. The second client would dislike a Pekingese who constantly sought her out. The first client would be upset with a dog who did not want to sleep with her in bed. Both dogs' behavior developed as a result of the feedback they received.

Effective communication requires a dialogue. Both parties must ask, listen, and respond at different times. The key is that the communication is reciprocal and empathic.

To teach a dog requires that you divide the behaviors you school into many small chunks of information. This way the dog's learning can progress in stages. He will not get overwhelmed with too much information, nor will he get so little information that he cannot figure out what to do. Although individual dogs differ in the amount of time spent at each stage, every dog follows three distinct learning stages:

1. The dog has no comprehension of what is expected.
2. The dog understands the idea intermittently.
3. The dog knows and performs on signal.

A dog starts learning when he makes choices based on information you have given him. For example, Sunny, a bichon frise, does not know how to lie down when asked. The word "down" does not have any meaning for her. It has not been associated with the necessary information and signals that will stimulate Sunny's ability to think of the behavior called "down."

Dogs lie down frequently. The difference is that Ann, Sunny's handler, wants her to lie down when Ann asks. In the beginning, Ann must show Sunny the physical response she expects. First, Ann asks Sunny to sit. Then, Ann uses a small dog biscuit to lure Sunny into a down position. Ann repeats this step until Sunny easily follows the lure and always lies down.

The second step associates the word signal "down" with the behavior. While Sunny follows the food lure and stretches out her front legs, Ann says "down." Ann stops practicing this step when she believes that Sunny has definitely tied the word "down" with the behavior of lying flat on the floor. The final step occurs when Ann says "down" without any food, and Sunny lies down instantly.

Using clear, consistent signals avoids confusion between you and your dog. Watch your word choice carefully. When Ken's young weimaraner jumped on the bed, he said "down!" The dog promptly lay flat on the bed. Ken really wanted to tell the dog "off." Off means "get off." Down means "lie down."

Dogs need time to process your requests. Say "down." If the dog does not respond instantly, wait for at least five seconds for the dog to respond. The space between your request for action and the dog's response is when a dog thinks and digests new information. Teaching dogs is a series of cognitive demands, and you need to allow time for the thinking process. However, you also need to give prompt feedback so that the dog experiences the consequences of his actions.

Timing is a critical factor when working with dogs. If you are too slow with your responses, the dog will not associate the particular behavior he performed with your reaction. You can also reward the incorrect response. For example, if you ask a dog to come to you, and then ask him to sit before you give him a reward, you reward the sit and not the come.

Timing is an art that requires you to acknowledge the link between a dog's behavior and your response. Learning when and what to respond to demands that you closely observe the dog's actions. A simple rule to follow is that the maximum time between a dog's response and a handler's reaction should be five seconds. Too many people assume that a dog misbehaves because the dog is stubborn, stupid, angry, or does not like them. Frequently, though, handlers, through poor timing, have not tied their response to the dog's behavior. Handlers should act like mirrors and allow dogs to "see" themselves through their reactions.

The bodyMIND approach to schooling dogs uses three techniques to communicate with dogs: rewards, redirections, and reprimands. Punishment has no place in the bodyMIND approach. Punishment occurs after the fact and often uses physical force to inflict varying degrees of pain in order to stop a behavior. Punishment does not give the dog an opportunity to choose a different option.

When dogs are punished, they may temporarily stop a behavior, but punishment does not teach dogs what specific behavior is desirable. In fact, dogs who are punished often associate the punishment with the presence of the handler rather than with the behavior. This results in dogs who chew, bark, or defecate, but only when the handler is not present or cannot reach them.

The primary response in the bodyMIND approach to schooling dogs is to *catch a dog doing something right* and then immediately reward the worthy behavior. All rewards are behavior-contingent and are timed so that a dog recognizes the particular behavior that earned a reward. When a dog knows the specific action he performed that earned the reward, he can repeat it.

Rewards are like green traffic lights. They tell dogs "keep it up," "I like that," and strengthen the right response. Rewards teach dogs they made the right choice. Most important, rewards are not the absence of punishment, but consist of food, sounds, touch, feelings, words, or activities.

Rewards can be as simple as a feeling of pride, words such as "You did great!," a soft sound like a hum, a higher pitch in your tone of voice, or a friendly rub. You can use any type of food—hot dogs, cheese, dog biscuits, popcorn, bread—anything dogs enjoy eating. Keep the size of a food reward small. All the dog needs is a taste, not dinner. Sometimes the best reward is an activity. For example, Red Sun Rising loves to walk in the park with his nose one inch above the grass searching for every smell. His favorite reward after we have worked on heeling, sit-stays, or dumbbell retrieves—all movements that require his attention on me and not on the ground—is to hear the words "go sniff." "Go sniff" frees Red to explore and discover any new scents since our last visit to the park.

Rewards can be combined. You can say "Good dog! I'm so proud of you!" and give the dog a small piece of hot dog. When dogs make a long-awaited breakthrough or perform a difficult maneuver easily, give them a jackpot reward. A jackpot reward is a whole handful of popcorn. Jackpots are big. You might clap, jump up and down, or give the dog a handful of food rewards as well as a friendly rub.

Rewards are signals that a dog has made the right choice. They are earned by dogs who offer specific behaviors. Rewards are not treats. Treats are given freely for any reason such as the dog looks "cute" and sharing banana bread with dogs makes you happy. Treats happen by chance or accident. Rewards depend on dogs performing specific actions to earn them.

In the beginning, when you teach a dog something new, reward the dog *every time* with his favorite food, ball, toy, or activity. Rewards are like paychecks. Most people would not work very long if they did not receive payment for their work. Dogs need paychecks too. However, once a dog associates a signal with a response and a reward, vary how often the dog receives his favorite food reward. Give the dog random food rewards that are strictly behavior-based. For example, if the dog sits when you say "sit," smile, but do not give the dog a food reward. On another occasion say "sit" and give the dog a friendly rub. Occasionally, after a sit, give the dog his favorite food reward. When your dog does not receive a food reward, always acknowledge his correct response through verbal praise, friendly rubs, or warm feelings.

Redirections are detours. They inform the dog that his current behavior is inappropriate and *at the same time* give the dog a better alternative. For example, the puppy is about to wet on the carpet. Instead of saying "no," the handler says "outside" in a lower-pitched voice with the inflection dropping at the end of the word. The tone of the handler's voice clues the dog in that this particular behavior is inappropriate. At the same time, "outside" presents the dog with a different option. "Outside" tells the dog to go outside and wet there.

With any problem behavior, look for another word signal that means the opposite, and teach it to the dog. For example, "gently" means do not grab the food from my hands; it opposes "take it." "Off" is contrary to "up." "Quickly" opposes "slowly." "Watch me" counters "look away." All redirections send a message that direct dogs to a different course of action.

Reprimands occur *during* a problem behavior. Like red stoplights, they tell dogs that their current activity must end. Reprimands do not teach but alert dogs that they made an incorrect decision. Reprimands attract a dog's attention so that the dog pauses and allows the handler to give a redirection. Reprimands consist of sounds, feelings, words, or interrupting activators such as spraying water.

Reprimands can be as simple as a feeling of disappointment, words such as "You have dishonored the pack, Mariah," a harsh sound like a whistle or a metal spoon on a pan, a lower pitch to your voice when you say "quit," or a squirt on a dog's nose from a squirt gun or a plant mister set on stream, not mist.

Reprimands can be combined. You can say "bad dog!" and combine it with a loud sound. However, reprimands are *never* physically abusive or punishing. If a dog ignores a reprimand, do not increase its intensity but try a different reprimand and go back to the basics. The issue is not disobedience. The problem is the dog does not understand. The dog's education is incomplete. Teach the dog to focus and pay attention to you. Then, teach the dog to sit, down, come, stay, or stand. Now, address the problem, if there still is one, after the reschooling.

Reprimands should be used sparingly. Resorting to reprimands means that the dog has not received the proper instruction in the first place. If you must reprimand, follow the one-a-day rule for reprimands: Do not correct a dog more than once a day with a reprimand. Too many nos diminish a dog's capacity to learn or perform, and damage your relationship. Instead, ignore the behavior, use redirections, or teach the dog a behavior that competes with the undesirable behavior and naturally eliminates it. For example, if a dog jumps on you when you come home, teach the dog to "sit." A dog cannot jump on you if he is sitting. If the dog runs out the door, teach the dog to "stay." A dog cannot run out the door if he is on "stay."

After any negative experience, do something positive. For example, praise the dog when he quits barking. Most important, whenever situations occur when the dog could bark but does not, reward him for making the correct choice.

This chapter contains some simple guidelines that I use successfully every day: Catch a dog doing something right, reward him; if a dog does something wrong, redirect him; if it is an emergency or there is no other option, reprimand him. However, these are only guidelines. Your teaching style determines how easily and quickly your dog learns.

Red Sun Rising just entered my office, laid his head on my lap, and sighed. I reach down, scratch between his eyebrows, and his eyes close. Like a miner in the Arizona desert, I have staked my claim, accepted my responsibility for Red's behavior, and am now reaping the rewards. No mystery there—just a dog, a woman, and their relationship, and that is what counts.

Part 3

THE PLAN:
Five Minutes a Day

CHAPTER 7

EXERCISING THE MIND:

Teaching Focus, Sit, Down, Walk, Stay, Come, Stand

Red Sun Rising, my golden retriever, streaks like a hawk after a mouse when he hears my whistle. Red knows the three-bar whistle means "come." Even if Red is in full chase after a rabbit or a cat, he stops and runs to me; not bad for a rescue dog who entered my life when he was ten months old. At ten months Red knew two things, running and jumping. In his previous home, someone had beaten him in the ribs with round-toed boots, shouted and yelled, jerked on his neck, and neglected to teach him to use the out-of-doors for his bathroom. In the beginning at my house, his idea of a good time was to devour a pillow off the couch, race through open doors, and use his sixty-five pounds to body-slam me and my husband in greetings. Red was a tornado whose energy dismantled anything in his path.

Today, Red Sun Rising bears no resemblance to that fractious, adolescent dog. The five-minute-a-day plan works, especially with dogs like Red who have excess energy and multiple problems. These techniques have also been used successfully on timid border collies, challenging German shepherds, excitable poodles, mild-mannered Great Danes, curious dachshunds, independent Shiba Inus, and many other breeds.

Teaching dogs to focus, sit, down, stay, stand, come, or walk by your side requires that you exit a world where spaghetti sauce comes in a jar, Jay Leno appears every weekday night in houses across the country, a blue Dodge pickup truck takes you to work or shopping, and visiting friends involves punching one, the area code, and seven numbers. Instead, you enter a dog's world where food is as close as the nearest garbage can, the scent of a wild rabbit spurs a long-distance chase, entertainment is digging for bones or chewing up shoes, and visiting friends involves fast escapes through open doors or over fences.

The secret to effective dog handling is to exercise your mind and not just your dog's body. Put on your detective's badge and ferret out the reasons behind your dog's behavior. Investigate his world. Find out what motivates your dog. Then, you can incorporate those motivators into your teaching program. Determine what stresses your dog. Then, you can eliminate or reduce unnecessary tension from his environment. Watch your dog and learn what natural cues elicit perfect sits, downs, comes, or stands.

The key words in the natural teaching process are when, what, where, why, and how. For example, before teaching your dog to sit, ask yourself, *when* during the normal course of a day does the dog sit? *Where* does he sit? *What* causes him to sit? *Why* does he stay in a sit? *How* do his muscles and bones operate so he can sit? The answers to these questions clue you in on the easiest way to teach your dog how to sit or any other natural behavior. Then, you can create situations that develop the dog's ability to think his way through each exercise.

Your daily interactions with your dog form the foundation of the five-minute-a-day plan. The dog's acceptance of you as teacher, companion, stranger or enemy influences his attentiveness to your requests. If your dog ignores you at home, he will not listen to you in the park. Your challenge is to build a relationship like a red-tailed hawk who comes home to rest on the arm of the falconer after free flight. Your dog listens to you because he cannot imagine being anywhere else.

When you work with your dog keep in mind the following nine elements to creating a successful schooling session:

1. Choose a safe, quiet, and calm location. Do not teach sit in the middle of the family room with the television blaring, the radio blasting, kids playing, family members eating, and other cats, dogs, gerbils, or birds loose and wandering through the house. Begin in an isolated room, porch, garage, or basement. If your dog has never been inside the house, work outside in the backyard during a quiet time of the day. As your dog learns each exercise, graduate to the backyard, the front yard, the neighbor's yard, or the park; move to different locations and increase the number and type of distractions present. However, change locations only after the dog has mastered the exercise in the current environment.

2. When you practice outside, attach a six-foot leash to the dog if you are not inside a fenced yard. You will need to hold on to the leash during the exercises, so that if something grabs the dog's attention he cannot chase after it.

3. Schedule the schooling sessions so that all the lessons occur before the dog eats and do not interfere with a regularly scheduled event. A dog's performance depends on his age, health, physical condition, time of day, season, and previous experiences.

4. Find out your dog's bodyMIND learning style so that you can tailor your lessons to his needs. Understanding your dog's bodyMIND attitude reduces your frustration and improves your dog's ability to learn. (See chapter 3 to determine your dog's bodyMIND attitude.)

5. Dogs learn faster with incentives. Use food, toys, balls, or activities as rewards when your dog offers an appropriate behavior. Rewards teach dogs which actions are correct.

- Place containers of dog biscuits, toys, or balls in your kitchen, living room, bedroom, and bathroom so you can instantly reward your dogs when you "catch them doing something right."
- In the beginning, always give your dog a physical reward. After your dog knows the behavior, vary how often he receives the physical reward. How-

ever, always recognize the dog's efforts in some way. For example, reward the dog with a friendly touch, a smile and a feeling of "I'm so proud of you," or the words "good dog!"

6. Start each schooling session by playing with your dog to stimulate and focus his attention on you. Then, take the same item you played with and use it as a motivator or a reward in the schooling session. For example, balls are wonderful motivators for dogs who are visually aware, stimulated by movement, excited by changing conditions, and seek out new events. Balls also promote interest and excitement in mellow dogs. Squeak toys easily motivate sound-sensitive dogs. Dog biscuits, cheese, hot dogs, popcorn, or any favorite food excite dogs who are smell sensitive. You can also use your body language as a motivator. You can jump up and down, wave your arms, spin in place, clap, or whistle.

Use your imagination and create games and motivators for your dog. Anything can build a dog's attention, interest, and enthusiasm, so study your dog and find out what appeals to him by watching him during his free time.

7. Teach your dog a "release" word. To "release" a dog requires that you teach the dog a signal that gives him permission to end his current activity. Choose a new word signal such as "okay," "free time," "release," "go play." Combine it with your body language: turn your back to the dog, clap your hands, raise your arms, or avert your eyes.

8. Practice each lesson from one to five times. Quit practicing before the dog becomes bored or inattentive.

Your session should always end with both of you wanting more.

9. Repeat the five-minute schooling session for as many days or weeks as necessary until the dog's response is completely automatic.

Focus

It is the last half of the ninth inning. Two outs. The score is tied and there is a runner on third base. The next batter is up and the count is two balls and one strike. The pitcher throws the ball too high. "Ball three," the umpire calls out. The batter waits. All eyes watch the pitcher's windup. As the ball speeds toward the batter, he swings and misses. "Strike two," the umpire says. The catcher throws the ball to the third baseman, but the runner returns in time. Meanwhile, the batter taps his cleats with the baseball bat, swings the bat in the air, and shifts his feet into the grass. The pitcher fires a fast ball. The batter swings, connects, and it's a home run over the right field fence. As the runners score, the crowd erupts in cheers, shouts, and whistles and streams onto the field.

No one tells a baseball player to keep his eyes on the ball. No one reminds the umpire the location of the strike zone. No one asks the spectators to watch what happens. Paying attention happens automatically.

Teaching a dog to focus is like playing baseball. Dogs are batters who learn that the difference between a home run and an empty swing depends on physical contact. Like a bat hitting a ball, focusing a dog's eyes on his handler takes practice, sharp reflexes, skill, ability, and patience.

Dogs watch handlers for four basic reasons:

1. The dog believes something good will happen to him.
2. The dog worries that something bad will happen to him.
3. The dog is not certain what will happen next.
4. The handler's actions excite the dog, and the dog wants to interact with the handler.

The playSMART approach recognizes that happy dogs learn faster because it builds on a dog's belief that something good will happen by using food, toys, and activities to reward the dog. Unexpected events and positive surprises maintain a dog's interest in paying attention. In addition, the handler's enthusiastic attitude and body language stimulate the dog's interest in focusing on the handler. When a dog is irresistibly attracted to something, he automatically focuses by watching you with his eyes, listening to your voice with his ears, and paying attention to you with his mind.

Test your dog's ability to focus on you with this simple exercise: Call the dog's name. Does the dog look at you, come to you, ignore you, or watch you until you release his attention?

If your dog comes to you, waits and watches, and glues his eyes to your every movement, move ahead to the next section and start schooling "sit." If the dog ignores you, looks steadily but does not come, or glances at you and then looks away, he needs to learn to pay attention *before* you work with him on any other exercise or behavior problem.

Lesson 1

The following steps build on a dog's natural inclination to focus when he is attracted to something.

Step 1. Put a small dog biscuit, piece of cheese, hot dog, or other food reward in your hand.

Step 2. While you stand in front of the dog, call the dog's name. Put the food between your lips.

Step 3. When the dog looks up, open your mouth. This allows the food reward to drop to the dog's upraised face.

HELP
If the dog stops watching you once he receives the reward, next time show him that you have two rewards before you give him his first reward.

Step 4. Repeat.

Step 5. Play with the dog.

HELP
If your dog is sight, sound, or movement sensitive, tuck a fleecy toy, squeak toy, or ball under your chin or hold it near your face. Then, lift your chin and allow it to roll down your chest and fall toward the dog's face.

Red focuses on the toy. JEFF CANTRELL

| 0:05 | *Lesson 2* |

1. Once the dog anticipates the reward, add a word signal such as "watch me," "focus," "up," "look," or "yo" before you release the reward. Any word signal is appropriate. Use one that is easy for you to remember.
2. When the dog watches you closely, increase the amount of time between when the dog focuses on you and when he receives his reward. Start with a two- or three-second delay, increase to six or seven seconds, wait for twelve seconds, and continue building his attention span. Never completely eliminate rewards, but let them happen at increasingly random intervals.
3. After one to five repetitions, play with your dog.

TEN-SECOND SESSION

During the day, anytime the dog looks at you, reward him with his favorite treat, ball, or toy.

Sit

Motorists who wait to make a left turn at a busy four-way intersection are like sitting dogs. A quick check left, a fast head turn right, an immediate look front, but no lucky breaks, so the driver waits. One pickup truck, a Civic, and a Detroit chrome mountain bearing down. Now, it is clear straight ahead. The Civic turned right.

The Oldsmobile passed. The driver hits the accelerator and speeds away. Drivers and dogs share one important trait. They sit and wait until their next move.

Mindy, a cocker spaniel, sits in front of closed doors while she waits for Beth to open them. Mindy sits patiently next to Beth's chair waiting for attention while Beth reads the newspaper. Mindy sits in the car to look out the window and lies down only when the car moves so fast the view outside the window blurs. When Beth stops at a traffic light or gas station, Mindy assumes her ready, sit, go position.

Dogs sit in anticipation of the next event. In a sit, folded back legs allow a dog's hindquarters to rest comfortably on the ground while upright front legs maintain a vertical position. Sitting allows dogs to wait comfortably, yet enables them to spring into action quickly. By understanding why dogs sit, you can structure situations that build on this natural sitting response.

Lesson 1

`0:05`

The following steps build on a dog's natural inclination to sit while he watches and waits.

Step 1. Face the dog.

Step 2. Place a small dog biscuit, piece of cheese, ball, toy, hot dog or other food reward in one hand.

Step 3. Hold the item over the dog's head just out of reach of the dog's mouth when he lifts up his muzzle in order to see it.

Hold the lure over the dog's head. JEFF CANTRELL

SeraJoy lowers her hindquarters. JEFF CANTRELL

SeraJoy sits. JEFF CANTRELL

Step 4. Move your hand slowly toward the dog's hindquarters. In order to follow the movement of your hand, the dog must lower his hindquarters.

Step 5. When the dog's hindquarters touch the ground, praise and reward the dog.

Step 6. Repeat.

Lesson 2

Step 1. After the dog lowers his hindquarters as a response to your moving hand, add the word signal "sit." Say "sit" while the dog's back legs are folding into position, *before* you give the dog the reward.

Step 2. Repeat.

Step 3. Now, hold the item over the dog's head, but do not move it. Say "sit." When the dog sits, reward him. If he does not sit, repeat the previous lesson.

Step 4. Repeat.

Lesson 3

Step 1. Hold the item approximately fifteen inches in front of the dog's face so he can see it in your hand. Say "sit." As soon as the dog's hindquarters rest on the ground, reward the dog.

Step 2. Repeat.

Step 3. Play with the dog.

Lesson 4

Step 1. Once the dog associates the lowering of his hindquarters with the word signal "sit" and a reward, ask the dog to sit without holding your hand in front of him. After he sits, reward him.

Step 2. Repeat.

Step 3. Play with the dog.

 TEN-SECOND SESSION 1

Incorporate asking the dog to sit into your daily routine. Ask the dog to sit before he eats his dinner, plays ball, or gets a friendly scratch. For example, if you ask the dog to sit before he eats, after he sits, release him. Say "okay," "free," "go eat your dinner," or any other appropriate phrase. Eating dinner after sitting is a wonderful food reward.

TEN-SECOND SESSION 2

Whenever you see the dog start to sit, say "sit." In the beginning, reward him with food or his favorite toy. If there is not a physical reward nearby, praise him or give him a rub if he enjoys touching.

TEN-SECOND SESSION 3

Once the dog learns he can sit and earn rewards, show him a favorite reward and ask "What are you going to do for this?" Wait. You are giving the dog the opportunity to think and perform

---

HELP

If your dog jumps instead of sits, you are holding the item too high over the dog's head. Lower the item until it almost touches the dog's head. Now, move the item toward the dog's hindquarters.

*a behavior to earn a reward. The dog may or may not sit right
away. Instead, he might bark, lay down, roll over, bring you a toy,
or other behaviors. Usually, after a short amount of time passes, he
will sit. When he does, praise and reward him.*

HELP
If your dog does not follow a dog biscuit, change to
a more appealing food, or try using a squeaky toy or
a ball. Make sure the dog likes what you hold in your
hand and *wants it now!*

HELP
If your dog follows the item but does not engage his
hindquarters, be patient. The dog does not know
what is expected of him. You may need to repeat
the initial head-to-hindquarters movement more
than once with your hand. Remember, a dog's
natural tendency is to sit while he waits, and you are
building on this response by holding something that
the dog wants out of reach above his head.

Down

Trevor, my twelve-year-old golden retriever, spends
80 percent of his time lying down. Even as a young dog,
Trevor's favorite position was full-body contact on the

floor. In front of the sliding-glass door at home he lies down to watch people, birds, and the occasional squirrel—events that would compel most dogs to move upright. Teaching Trevor the signal "down" required only a few thirty-second sessions. Even Ginger, a high-energy boxer, took only a few minutes to learn down. Yet teaching down frustrates many people because factors such as the dog's comfort or safety level, acceptance of authority, and environment play important, yet hidden, roles.

Normally, dogs lie down when they feel safe and nothing requires an immediate response. Depending on the dog, he might lie on his back, stretch out flat with his stomach on the floor, rest on his side, or crouch. (In a crouch the dog looks like he is lying down, but there is not complete contact between the dog and the floor.) Dogs lie down when they wait, rest, sleep, or are sick. Some dogs lie and wait before they spring up and pounce on their victims.

A dog's survival is based on his ability to attack or flee from danger. In a down position, the dog loses an important psychological advantage. He appears smaller, less menacing, and assumes a traditional subservient position. His range of vision is reduced substantially. In addition, the dog loses a strategic physical advantage; valuable seconds can disappear before a dog can stand, flee, or fight.

All downs are not the same. There is a big difference between a dog who lies down randomly during the day and a dog who lies down at the handler's request. A dog who lies down upon request, under any conditions, accepts and trusts his handler completely.

The playSMART approach uses food, toys, and balls to teach down. It avoids the contest of wills that happens when handlers use physical force to push or pull a dog into position. Dogs react to force by resisting. If dogs view lying down as a battle for top dog position, they often resist, struggle, or fight. If they submit, they tune out mentally.

0:05 — *Lesson 1*

In the beginning, I teach dogs to lie down from the sit because in the sit the dog's hindquarters already touch the ground. In order to lie down, the dog only needs to stretch out his front legs to make full-body contact with the floor. The following steps build on a dog's natural inclination to lie down when he feels safe. Instead of a play activity, begin this session by spending some quiet time with your dog.

Step 1. Place a small dog biscuit, piece of cheese, ball, toy, hot dog, or other reward in your hand.

Step 2. Face the dog. Sink down on your haunches.

Step 3. Hold your hand in front of the dog's nose. Let him sniff the food. If you are using a toy or ball, wave your hand in front of his nose, or squeak the toy.

Step 4. With the toy in your hand, draw a line from the dog's nose to the ground between his front paws. Go slowly enough so the dog can follow your hand, but not so slowly he loses interest.

Hold the lure in front of the dog. JEFF CANTRELL

Step 5. When you reach the ground draw your hand toward you. (You are drawing the letter "L" in the air.) If the dog's nose follows your hand, he will stretch out his front legs while you pull your hand back.

HELP
If the dog does not follow the lure in your hand, change the item until you find something that the dog really wants.

Draw the lure down to Rocky's paws. JEFF CANTRELL

HELP

If the dog stands up and walks over to you, move the lure slower so that it is easier for the dog to follow and catch it. If moving the lure slower does not help, try covering the lure with your hand after you pull the lure about one foot in front of the dog. Some dogs lay down in order to paw it.

Another option, if you use food as your lure, is to give the dog a small bite of food as he stretches his body while he follows your hand. For example, after he lowers his head a couple of inches, feed him. Move your hand a few inches, let him follow it, and feed him. Repeat until he stretches out completely.

Step 6. As soon as the dog's body touches the floor, praise and reward him.

Step 7. Ask the dog to sit, and repeat the exercise.

Step 8. Play with the dog.

Rocky lays down. JEFF CANTRELL

Lesson 2

| 0:05 |

Step 1. When the dog automatically lowers his body to the ground into a down position by following the lure in your hand, add the word signal "down." Say "down" as the dog's front legs stretch out in front of him, *before* you give the dog the reward.

Step 2. Repeat.

Step 3. Play with the dog.

| 0:05 | *Lesson 3* |

Step 1. Hold the item in front of the dog, but do not move it. Say "down." When the dog lies down, reward him. If he does not lie down, practice more with the lure.

Step 2. Repeat.

Step 3. Play with the dog.

TEN-SECOND SESSION 1

Whenever you see your dog start to lie down, say "down." In the beginning, reward him with food or his favorite toy. If there is not a physical reward nearby, praise him or give him a rub if he enjoys touching.

TEN-SECOND SESSION 2

Hold a lure (food, squeak toy, or ball) under a chair or end table so the dog has to lay down in order to reach it. As the dog lies down say "down." Praise and reward him.

Walk

Walking a dog is like trying to catch an ocean wave with separated fingers. Water spills through, buffets your hands, and sprays your face. The elusive wave avoids your grasp. Instead, its undertow grabs you for a ride. You spin in its grip. Pulling against it, straining arms cannot contain the wave's force and you sink beneath its weight. Dogs, like ocean waves, can drag and

Using the playSTICK with SeraJoy. JEFF CANTRELL

pull us when we use bare hands and muscles as our tools.

Asking dogs to walk without dragging us in their wake requires that we use new ideas, tools, and methods, because walking with a person is not a natural behavior for dogs. Dogs explore, roam, and seek out new smells, places, and other animals. Their natural behavior is to track, hunt, shadow, unearth, ferret, and inquire into forgotten places and hidden spaces. Yet trips to the veterinarian, groomer, park, or pet store demand a dog's close proximity to our side.

Walking is not heeling. Heeling is a behavior that is required in dog show rings where a dog's head/shoulder area must line up with the handler's left hip at all times. "Walking" means a dog stays close to the handler's side, does not pull, but is not riveted to the handler's left leg and can shift position.

Lesson 1

`0:05`

Have you ever wondered why dogs have trouble understanding how to walk next to us quietly and closely, with no tugging or pulling? Dogs focus on what happens in front of them. When handlers ask a dog to walk next to them, there is nothing to guide the dog except the contact with the collar or the lure of a future reward. However, some dogs do not respond to lures. Besides, lures are not always practical with small dogs like terriers or spaniels, since human backs cannot always bend in the pretzel shape required to hold a lure in front of a small dog's nose.

When I realized that a dog's eyes focus on what they see, and a dog's body responds to what his eyes observe, I knew I had discovered the secret to teaching dogs how to walk without pulling my arms from their sockets, or walking on my knees to teach a West Highland white terrier to stick close. That is when I started using a playSTICK.

Dogs pay attention to what they see, and a play-STICK acts as an extension to a handler's arm. Most dogs are movement or sight sensitive, and they respond quickly to the playSTICK's presence in front of their face. In the same way a conductor uses a baton to lead an orchestra, a playSTICK shows a dog what to do. Dogs see "hand" signals in front of their eyes. By waving the playSTICK like a fan or pointing it, the playSTICK guides a dog, no matter how tall or short he is. Using a playSTICK is very effective with movement- and sight-sensitive dogs, canines with short attention spans and memories, and dogs who lack confidence and stress easily.

A playSTICK can be made out of anything. You can use a dowel rod, old curtain bar, broom handle, yard-stick, arrow (without the point), umbrella, or even a fairly straight tree branch. Once when I did not have a playSTICK with me, I used a long, narrow, leaf frond. Find a playSTICK light enough so you can grip it softly with your hand and does not strain your arm to carry it.

Never use a playSTICK to hit your dog.

Hold the playSTICK at a 45-degree angle and carry it ten to sixteen inches in front of the dog's face while you are walking. (If the playSTICK is too close to the dog's face, he cannot see it. If it is too far away, the dog can ignore it.) There are three basic ways to use the playSTICK:

- Wave it like a fan
- Tap it on the dog's body like your hand
- Or sweep it in front of the dog like opening a door

Use the playSMART approach and make a game out of teaching your dog to follow the playSTICK. Dogs who focus their attention on a playSTICK ignore potential distractions and pull less. Try this:

Step 1. Find a quiet space and teach your dog to follow the playSTICK with his eyes. Hold the playSTICK six inches in front of the dog's nose. If your dog touches it with his nose, praise and reward him. Repeat.

Step 2. Move the end of the playSTICK three or four inches in front of the dog's nose. Wiggle it. Bounce it up and down. When the dog follows it, praise and reward him. Repeat.

HELP

If your dog does not inspect it, get the dog's attention. Take a favorite food treat and wiggle it just behind the playSTICK. Entice the dog to come forward. When he touches the playSTICK with his nose, give him the food treat. Repeat.

HELP
If your dog does not follow the playSTICK, rub cheese, sandwich spread, or peanut butter on it to lure the dog to follow it. Repeat Lesson 1.

Step 3. Once the dog follows the playSTICK with his eyes, you are ready to introduce your dog to the "walk" signal.

Lesson 2

0:05

Begin this exercise in a space that is large enough for you to walk ten feet in one direction such as a living room, great room, hallway, basement, or garage. After your dog masters the current space, move to different locations.

Attach the leash to the dog's collar. Carry the leash in your right hand. Do not wrap the leash around your hand but fold the leash in layers like an accordion inside your hand. Keep a light contact between your leash hand and the dog's collar. You cannot pull a dog into position! The dog must choose to walk with you. Make sure the free end of the leash does not drop down and wave in front of the dog's eyes.

Step 1. Stand with the dog at your left side. Hold the playSTICK in your right hand.

Lightly tap the dog's chest with the playSTICK. LINDA BRUCE

Step 2. Introduce the "sweep." Lightly tap the dog's chest with the end of the playSTICK. Like opening a door, move the playSTICK from the dog's chest to approximately one foot in front of the dog. At the same time, walk forward with your left foot. Dogs follow movement, so when the playSTICK sweeps in front of him, the dog automatically moves into the opening it creates, like a water-skier pulled by a boat.

Step 3. Say "walk" while you "sweep" the playSTICK in front of the dog and step forward with your left foot. Praise the dog when he moves with you.

Step 4. Introduce the "wave." If the dog starts pulling or moving in front of you, take the playSTICK and "wave" it up and down vertically in front of the dog's face, from four to eight inches below the dog's head to four to eight inches above his head. Whenever you wave the playSTICK, move it vertically down toward the earth and up toward the sky.

(Lesson continued on page 141)

HELP

If the dog still wants to tug, at the same time you wave the playSTICK, give a slight tug-and-release with your leash hand. As soon as the dog slows down, praise and reward him.

You can also lightly touch the dog's chest and then "wave" the playSTICK. This combination slows dogs down because the movement of the playSTICK inhibits their forward momentum.

Sweep the playSTICK in front of the dog. LINDA BRUCE

Tap the dog with the playSTICK on the shoulder. LINDA BRUCE

Tap the dog with the playSTICK on the hip. LINDA BRUCE

Step 5. Introduce the "tap." If the dog pulls away from your left side, "tap" the playSTICK *lightly* on the dog's outside/left shoulder or hip while you walk. You can also "wave" the playSTICK along the left side of the dog's body. Or, plan your session so that you walk with a wall on your left side. Then, the dog must stay close to your left leg.

Step 6. If the dog crowds your left leg, "wave" the playSTICK between your leg and the dog's body to encourage the dog to keep some distance between the two of you.

Step 7. After one or two minutes, play with the dog.

Step 8. Repeat the previous steps.

Lesson 3

`0:05`

Step 1. Add left turns, right turns, and about turns to your walk. Any time you turn, say the dog's name and repeat the word "walk." If a dog lags on a turn, run. Walk around trees, swing sets, or garbage bins. If your working area is empty of obstacles, create them. Fill one-gallon milk cartons with water or sand and place five of them in a straight line six feet apart. Start by walking around the milk cartons, then change your pace. Go fast, slow, and normal. Obstacles force a dog to listen and pay attention to you.

Step 2. Change your tempo. Walk slowly for ten steps and return to your normal pace. Run quickly for ten feet and return to your normal pace. Skip. Let the dog adjust his pace to yours.

Step 3. Next, add circles of different sizes to your walk. Walk a small left circle, then walk a large left circle. Walk straight, then add a large right circle. Change the number of times you follow a circle. For example, walk a medium right circle twice, then walk straight ahead. Turn left, then walk a small left circle three times. Change directions by making a small half-circle.

Step 4. Repeat walking, stopping, and making circles. Keep your routine from becoming predictable. Walk over plastic, around paper bags, or through tree branches on the ground. Run, skip, or move slowly. Build on a dog's natural anticipation of what will come next, and surprise him into listening to your signals.

If you want to use a lure instead of a playSTICK to teach your dog to walk quietly by your side, follow these steps.

Circling to the left is an easy way to keep a dog from pulling on his leash. Since the dog is on your left, when you walk a small four-foot circle to the left, it stops the dog's forward momentum because your left leg crosses in front of him. The dog hesitates to avoid hitting your leg. Never hit a dog with your leg, just move faster than the dog so that he automatically slows down.

Lesson 1

Step 1. Place a small dog biscuit, piece of cheese, ball, toy, hot dog, or other food reward in your left hand.

Red follows the food lure. JEFF CANTRELL

Step 2. Stand with the dog on your left side. Hold the lure with your left hand in front of the dog's nose so he can smell it, see it, or hear it. If you use food, make sure the food is something the dog really likes to eat. Rest your elbow on your hip so that your hand stays next to your leg. If you have a small dog, bend over and hold your arm straight so that the dog can smell the food.

Step 3. Lead with your left foot and walk two or three steps while holding the lure in front of the dog's nose. Encourage the dog to sniff it. Praise him as he follows the lure. Give the dog the reward after the third step.

Step 4. Repeat. Walk another three or four steps before giving the dog the reward.

Step 5. While the dog walks next to your side, add the word signal "walk." Use a happy, enthusiastic voice. Do not stop when you say "walk"—keep moving. After a few steps reward the dog.

Step 6. Repeat. Vary the number of steps you walk before the dog receives the reward.

Step 7. Play with the dog.

Lesson 2

This exercise is identical to the previous exercise, except the leash is attached to the dog's collar.

Step 1. Attach the leash to the dog's collar. Carry the leash in your right hand. Do not wrap the leash around your hand but fold the leash in layers like an accordion inside your hand. Keep a light contact between your leash hand and the dog's collar. You cannot pull a dog into position! The dog must choose to walk with you. Make sure the free end of the leash does not drop down and wave in front of the dog's eyes.

Step 2. Hold the food lure in your left hand and walk three steps. Praise and reward. Walk five steps. Praise and reward. Vary the number of steps you walk before the dog receives the reward.

Step 3. Practice walking, praising, rewarding, stopping, and walking. Change the number of steps you take each time.

Step 4. Play with the dog.

HELP
If a dog lags behind you, do not slow down to wait for him. Bring along a toy or ball and use it as a lure. Toss it in front of you. Chase it. Get the dog excited about what you are doing. Play and then walk a few steps. Repeat.

Stay

On Saturday afternoon the line at the bank stretched to the door. I know: My back was against the ten-foot glass pane. As I stood there watching, I heard the bank teller explain to the man in the blue cap, denim shirt, and oil-stained jeans that the computer went down and sorting out the overdraft problem in his checking account would take longer than normal. My first thought was I did not have time for this delay. My second thought was this was a perfect time to watch how people handle a stay signal.

The young girl in shorts and a midi-top started tapping her foot and playing with the silver chain around her neck. A lady in a cream business suit searched through her purse, pulled out a book, and started reading. An older couple dressed in tuxedo T-shirts saying "Arizona suits us fine" discussed their upcoming trip to Sedona. Other people in the line shifted their feet, swung their arms, and stared out the windows at the bank's parking lot. After four minutes people started muttering to each other, saying things like, "Do you believe it?" "I don't have time to stand here all day." "Why is there only one teller?" One man's face turned bright red, and he slammed the door on his way out saying, "This is ridiculous, I have things I need to do."

I thought how dogs must have some of the same feelings when we ask them to stay. Time hangs. They are asked to wait passively when there are rabbits to chase, dogs to play with, UPS carriers to bark at, and children to greet. No wonder dogs get up and leave, sniff the grass, or greet their neighbors when we ask them to stay.

Teaching stay is not, as most people think, a test of the amount of control a handler exerts over a dog. Instead, the stay signal asks dogs to develop patience, a quality that is missing in many people. Patience is a virtue, and dogs, like people, encounter situations when they must bide their time. Dogs stay while their handler stops and talks with neighbors during walks. Dogs wait while their handler jogs in place at traffic lights, opens the house door, or brings them to the veterinarian's waiting room.

The bodyMIND approach capitalizes on a dog's ability to think, builds on the dog's natural capacity to wait, and proves to a dog that staying only delays his ability to run, chase, explore, or flee, but does not permanently inhibit it. There is no doubt in my mind who controls a stay. The handler cannot prevent a dog from moving; dogs control their own nerves, muscles, and bones.

During the course of a day, dogs stay naturally when they are tired, resting, sleeping, waiting, bored, or sick. When dogs alert to threatening noises or commotions, muscles quiver, hackles raise, and they wait motionless until the coast is clear or the disturbance enters their territory. Often, dogs adopt frozen positions before they pounce on unsuspecting chipmunks, birds, or rabbits.

A proper stay occurs when a dog remains in one location upon signal. For most people, the signal should be called "place" rather than "stay." Immovable stays are necessary in dog show rings, but "place" is perfect for family dogs where it does not matter if the dog changes from sit to down or rolls over on his side, as long as he remains in one spot.

As soon as a dog learns to sit or down, he can learn to stay. Teaching place requires a search for situations, items, or actions that develop a dog's ability to wait.

Dogs stay when the incentive to stay is stronger than the desire to move. Place needs to increase a dog's patience, not amplify his boredom. Only use a place signal when you are physically near a dog and working with him. Never tell a dog "place" before you leave the house.

Practice the place exercise during times when you feel quiet and relaxed, and when there are no distractions to interrupt you or interfere with the dog. During the beginning sessions, keep your attention focused on the dog. Do not chat with other people, fidget, or fiddle with your hands. I pretend that roots grow out of my feet into the ground to keep me motionless. Use this time to breathe softly and deeply. Release any tension from your shoulders, neck, and back. Relax, and send those feelings to your dog.

Lesson 1

`0:05`

Begin by using Animal Energetics to relax your dog. Chapter 9 covers the different Animal Energetics techniques.

Step 1. Stand in front of, or next to, the dog. Ask the dog to sit, lay down, or remain standing. Choose the dog's favorite position.

"Place" hand signal in front of Trevor. LINDA BRUCE

Step 2. Say "place." At the same time, drop your outstretched hand, palm side toward the dog, three inches in front of the dog's face for three seconds. Return your hand to your side.

Step 3. If the dog remains motionless, praise him quietly. Do not move away from him. If the dog moves at any point during the stay exercise, do not yell but calmly reach over, return the dog to his previous stay position, and say "place." If you stand in front of the dog, do not stare at him. You can look at the dog briefly, or gaze at his body or what is near him, but staring often signals a dog to come to you.

Practicing place on a board with Molly. LINDA BRUCE

Step 4. Wait four or five seconds. Praise and reward the dog. Use food as your reward rather than toys or balls so the dog does not move until you give the release signal.

Step 5. Release your dog from place. Say "okay," "release," or "free."

Your next action after saying "release" depends on the bodyMIND learning style of your dog. If the dog has a high PAR (see page 17) level, after you say "release," bend down, scratch, rub, but most important, soothe the dog for a short time before you ask the dog to play with you.

If the dog has a lower PAR level, play with the dog immediately. Try to bounce the dog out of stay by clapping your hands, whistling, using a happy and excited voice, running, or jumping, so that the dog learns that waiting patiently precedes playtime.

Step 6. Repeat the previous steps. Wait another three or four seconds. Release the dog.

HELP

If you have an active dog who finds it impossible to remain in one location, place on the ground a rug, towel, cardboard, or plywood sheet that is larger than the dog's sitting or flat body position. Practice place on this surface. If the dog leaves this space, place a plywood board on cement blocks and ask the dog to stay on this mini-platform.

Lesson 2

Step 1. Repeat the stay-and-reward sequence, in the previous lesson. Increase the amount of time by five-second intervals before you reward your dog.

To decrease any boredom the dog might be feeling in a longer stay, change your behavior while the dog waits. For example, turn around slowly in place, wait for ten seconds, and turn around again. Wait for five seconds and release the dog.

Step 2. Play with the dog.

Step 3. Repeat the stay and reward sequence.

Lesson 3

When the dog stays quietly for thirty seconds with you in front of him or next to him, increase your distance from the dog.

Step 1. Say "place." Wait ten seconds. Then, move one step away from the dog. The dog will look up when you move. If the dog moves out of position, do not yell at him but calmly walk over, return the dog to his previous stay position, and say "place." Wait ten seconds and move one step again. If the dog remains in position, praise him quietly.

Slowly increase the distance from your dog in three-foot increments until you can leave your dog

Move one step away. LINDA BRUCE

twenty feet away, and he stays while you bend over to tie your shoes, bounce up and down, drop to your knees, sit on the ground, pivot on one foot and turn in a circle, turn your back to him, lay on the ground, talk to your kids, gesture, or any other potentially distracting behaviors.

Step 2. Return to the dog. Step back to your original position and praise and reward the dog.

Step 3. Move two steps away from your dog. Wait for five, ten, or fifteen seconds.

Drop on your knees. LINDA BRUCE

Step 4. Return to the dog. Reward and release him.

Step 5. Play with the dog.

TEN-SECOND SESSION 1

During the day when you see your dog lying down completely relaxed and comfortable, stand near him and say "place." After ten seconds praise, release, and play with him.

Sit with your back to the dog. LINDA BRUCE

TEN-SECOND SESSION 2
Signal the dog to place while you throw a ball or toy for him to retrieve. At first, you may have to hold on to the dog's collar, but after a short amount of time he will wait for you to throw the ball.

TEN-SECOND SESSION 3
Incorporate place sessions during your daily routine. For example, practice place during television commercials, while you wash dishes, or when you take out the garbage or iron clothes.

Come

Rams, a six-year-old saluki, hurtled through space in hot pursuit of a rabbit, like a sidewinder missile locked onto the tailpipes of a MiG-29. Jeff, my husband, shouted "come." Four white paws stopped in mid flight as Rams leapt in the air, spun, and launched himself in our direction. With one microsecond to impact, he dropped at my husband's feet. Dogs, like SMART missiles, execute instructions they know.

When dogs come when you call, you can take them anywhere. Dogs who come can run free in the woods, at the beach, or in the park. In addition, dogs who come avoid potentially dangerous situations by listening to their handlers and not entering a street full of traffic or joining a dog fight.

On the surface, come appears to be a simple behavior; the dog leaves his present site and joins you at a different location. In reality, come is a highly complicated maneuver. Come requires that the dog responds to you over his natural interests and instincts.

The best way to teach come is to think about it from a dog's point of view. A dog investigates whatever stimulates his interest, such as enticing smells, unusual sounds, new people or animals, or moving objects. You cannot bribe or force a dog to come. Instead, you need to convince your dog that you are more important than anything else.

Luckily, dogs spontaneously come to us many times during a normal day. My dogs race to greet me at the door when I return home after an absence. When I am at home, they search me out when I open the patio door or cook in the kitchen. When my dogs find me, I reward them with scratches, toys, biscuits, or playtime. I want them to know when they choose me, they earn rewards. I never ask a dog to come and then clip the dog's nails, give him a bath, or yell or punish him. Instead, I teach the dog that whenever he comes, something nice happens.

Lesson 1

```
0:05
```

Start teaching come inside the house. The key to this behavior is to practice, practice, practice until it becomes a response so deeply ingrained in your dog that he pays attention to you anywhere.

Begin this exercise in a space that is large enough for you to walk ten feet in one direction such as a living room, great room, hallway, basement, or garage.

Step 1. Play with the dog. Use one of his favorite

toys. I use squeak toys because they stimulate a dog's sight, hearing, and movement senses. If your dog does not like squeak toys but loves pull toys, use those to play with him. The point is for the dog to be interested in you. If that requires that you bounce up and down, wave your arms, clap your hands, whistle, or use food as a lure, do it.

Step 2. Once you have captured the dog's attention, back away three or four steps from him, squeak the toy, wave the pull toy, wiggle the food, and crouch down. As the dog runs toward you, back up a few more steps.

Step 3. When the dog "catches" you, praise and reward him.

Sunny catches me. JEFF CANTRELL

Step 4. Repeat. This time as soon as the dog runs toward you say "come." Use a happy, enthusiastic voice. When he comes, praise and reward him.

Lesson 2

`0:05`

Step 1. Use the playSMART approach and turn come into a game. Ask someone to hold the dog while you run into another room. Call the dog's name, say "come," and let the dog find you.

Step 2. When the dog "catches" you, praise and reward him.

Step 3. Move to different locations throughout the house. Hide behind doors, beds, furniture, or in a closet with an open door. Always praise and reward the dog when he finds you.

Once your dog *always* comes when you call him inside the house, you can move your lessons outside.

Lesson 3

`0:05`

Find a fenced area for this next session. If your backyard is fenced, great. If not, borrow a neighbor's or a friend's yard. Working the dog without a leash forces you to attract the dog's attention.

Step 1. Bring two tennis balls, squeak toys, or two small sealed sandwich Baggies filled with dog biscuits. Place one item in your hand and put the other item in a pocket. Let the dog see the ball, squeak toy, or dog biscuits. Play with the dog. Then, throw the item away from where the two of you are playing.

Step 2. Tell the dog to "get it," "fetch," or any signal you choose that means "go after the item now."

HELP
If you cannot find a fenced area, attach a twenty-foot lightweight leash or line to your dog's collar so he can run but you can stop him if he leaves the area. Remember, the leash's purpose is only to prevent runaways or accidents. Do not use the leash to pull the dog toward you. In the beginning, hold the leash in your hands as you play with the dog and he runs for the ball. Next, let the dog drag the leash on the ground. Then, change to a short, twelve-inch-long tab leash instead of a long leash. Remember, the dog must have a rock-solid response before you change to a short tab leash.

Step 3. As soon as the dog grabs the item, call the dog's name. Start playing with the second item. Bounce the ball, squeak the toy, or toss the dog biscuit up and down in your hands, and pretend to eat from it. If necessary, jump up and down, clap your hands, and entice the dog to come to you. When the dog moves toward you, say "come." As soon as the dog starts heading your way praise him.

Step 4. Crouch down low. Back up a few steps. Keep wiggling and squeaking the item.

Step 5. When the dog reaches you, reward him.

Step 6. Repeat.

Step 7. Play with your dog.

During future lessons, increase the type and number of distractions in the dog's environment. For example, ask your children to play in the yard, or find someone to ride by on a bike or walk in front of your house with another dog on-leash.

TEN-SECOND SESSION 1

Whenever your dog runs toward you during the day, say "come" just before he reaches you. Then, praise and reward him.

TEN-SECOND SESSION 2

Before mealtime, call your dog. Say the dog's name first and then "come." Then, feed the dog his meal.

TEN-SECOND SESSION 3

At any time, ask the dog to come. Praise and reward him. Then, let the dog return to whatever he was doing.

HELP
If your dog runs past you, run in the opposite direction so that the dog starts chasing you. Give the dog another signal such as sit or down. Spread your legs wide in a V shape and throw the ball, toy, or food between your legs just before the dog reaches you so that he will dart through your legs chasing the item.

HELP
If your dog is not motivated by toys, balls, or food, change your body language. For example, lie down on the ground, roll over, kneel down, hide your head in your hands and make strange noises, whistle, or clap before you ask the dog to come. If you know your dog's bodyMIND learning style, you can easily find something to interest and excite your dog.

Stand

When your training time is filled with teaching focus, sit, stay, down, and come, it is easy to overlook the importance of the stand exercise. Yet, I ask my dogs to stand frequently. Stand is an important behavior that dogs use during grooming, bathing, visiting the veterinarian, cleaning feet on rainy or snowy days, or with the Mountain and Rainbow techniques in the Animal Energetics work (see Chapter 9).

When dogs adopt a motionless upright position on four legs, you can assume that their eyes, nose, or ears have discovered something that bears further investigation. Dogs stand when their fear, fight, or freeze instincts are aroused. They stand until they decide what to do next. Dogs also stand when something prevents them from moving forward and blocks their path, such as a door, window, gate, or hand.

A significant portion of any dog's time is spent standing, so teaching a dog how to stand is relatively simple. By using food, squeak toys, or crinkly paper as lures, you can capitalize on a dog's naturally inquisitive nature.

Lesson 1

`0:05`

Step 1. Put a small dog biscuit, piece of cheese, hot dog, squeak toy, or ball in your right hand.

Step 2. Ask the dog to sit at your left side. Crouch or stand next to him.

Step 3. Place your right hand, with the item, in front of his nose. Encourage the dog to sniff the food or toy.

Step 4. Wiggle your hand in front of the dog's face and pull it away from the dog. As the dog stands up,

Hold a lure in your hand to attract the dog's attention.

Encourage the dog to sniff the item.

Draw your hand away from the dog's face. JEFF CANTRELL

SeraJoy stands. JEFF CANTRELL

praise and reward him. If the dog remains sitting, repeat the previous step.

Step 5. If the dog's hindquarters remain firmly planted on the ground, place your left hand under the dog's stomach. Then, as you pull your right hand away, your left hand gently supports the dog and lifts him into a stand.

Step 6. Say "stand," as the dog unfolds his back legs and adopts the standing position.

Step 7. Do not move but remain by the dog's side. Wait five seconds. Then, praise and reward.

Step 8. Release the dog.

Step 9. Repeat the previous steps.

Step 10. Play with the dog.

TEN-SECOND SESSION

During the day whenever you see your dog standing motionless, say "stand." Praise, release, and reward him.

CHAPTER **8**

DEVELOPING YOUR NATURAL POTENTIAL

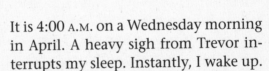 It is 4:00 A.M. on a Wednesday morning in April. A heavy sigh from Trevor interrupts my sleep. Instantly, I wake up. I cannot see Trevor, but I can hear the rattle in Trevor's chest as he steals one more breath from overworked lungs. Gently, I slip out from under the bed covers so that my husband's sleep will not be disturbed.

Searching in the dark I find Trevor lying on the bathroom floor. I lower myself next to him saying, "Hi Trevor, it's Animal Energetics time again. I heard your call." Before I begin Trevor's session, I steady my heartbeat by taking soft, deep, regular breaths, relax my hands, and wait for "*chi*" (pronounced "chee"), the universal life energy, to enter them.

My shoulders relax, my breathing sinks to my diaphragm, and the *chi* energy pulses in my hands Now, I am ready to practice Animal Energetics. Fifteen minutes later the session is over. Trevor's breathing is deeper; his muscles have relaxed, and the rattle in his throat is not as harsh. The valley fever that has attacked Trevor's lungs is held at bay again.

Valley fever is an insidious disease of the Southwest that attacks a dog's lungs, bones, joints, or organs. Although medication helps, older dogs like Trevor cannot rid their bodies of its effects. Animal Energetics eases the congestion in Trevor's lungs by increasing the flow of the energy meridians inside his body.

Energy exists inside every living organism. It is an organic substance that has many names. The Chinese name it *"chi"*; Indians describe it as *"prana"*; westerners refer to it as "energy"; and Luke Skywalker in the *Star Wars* trilogy called it "the Force." To me, this invisible field is similar to electricity. When I turn on a light, I do not see an electric current coursing through wires to reach the tungsten filament inside a light bulb, but the current is there.

In the same way that electricity is carried through wires, *chi* circulates through twelve principal energy meridians or pathways inside a dog's body. Meridians are rivers of energy that flow through joints, bones, muscles, and organs.

The practice of Animal Energetics uses a person's mind and hands to direct and release this invisible organic energy in order to soften muscles, release tight nerves, activate dormant areas, and stimulate a dog's relaxation response.

Practicing Animal Energetics requires that we connect our mind and body so that our hands receive, release, and direct energy clearly without any emotional or mental "baggage." For example, if you just finished fighting with your supervisor, the neighbor, or your kids, do not start an Animal Energetics session. When you are anxious or stressed, it diminishes the effectiveness of an Animal Energetics session. You can also transfer your aches, pains, and stresses to the dog, since your hands are an extension of your mind. However, if your mind is clear and you feel quiet and peaceful, a dog can draw strength from you, relax, feel better, and learn more easily.

Animal Energetics does not replace veterinarians. The first person to visit if your dog is in physical trouble is your veterinarian. However, once the veterinarian has diagnosed the problem and established treatment, using Animal Energetics in conjunction with veterinary care speeds a dog's recovery.

Animal Energetics accesses the invisible energy inside dogs, releasing fear, pain, anger, sorrow, anxiety, and other mental and emotional tensions that dogs store in their bodies—tensions that can cause disease, dysfunction, or problem behaviors. Stressed dogs lick excessively, bark, dig, mouth, bite, chew, or act hyper, nervous, or depressed. They soil in the house, jump, pull on their leashes, and have trouble learning how to sit, come, or stay.

Traditional training has limits. How does knowing how to sit change a dog's desire to chew? How does learning down help a dog feel comfortable with nail clipping, thunderstorms, or riding in cars? If a dog has been abused, how does heeling teach a dog to trust people?

Animal Energetics develops your sensitivity and skills so that you can use it with your dogs and validate it for yourself. The following exercises introduce you to a series of movements to improve your ability to quiet your mind, relax your body, feel energy, and connect with an energy field that protects you and your dog.

Exercise 1: Freeing Trapped Thoughts

This exercise explores your body, one part at a time, and relaxes tight muscles, frayed nerves, and constricted veins. Like peeling an onion, you strip away any physical or mental tensions.

Try this:

1. Assume a standing position. Let your hands hang by your sides.
2. Separate your feet until the distance between your feet equals the width of your shoulders. Keep your feet parallel and bend your knees slightly.
3. Close your eyes. Your mind, not your eyes, searches for any tight places inside your body.
4. Breathe softly. Inhale slowly. With each breath allow your shoulders to gently rise; feel how your lungs expand and your chest rises.
5. With each exhale, allow your shoulders to fall; feel how the air leaves your lungs and your chest sinks.

6. Allow your shoulders to keep rhythm with your breathing, rising when you inhale and lowering when you exhale. Imagine clear water flowing through you, removing sore muscles, achy joints, and tight spots in your mind.

7. Start at your head and relax your facial muscles, jaw, and neck. Smile.

8. Then, relax your chest, stomach, and back. Sigh.

9. Stretch your arms and legs. Feel your feet pushing against the floor. Yawn.

10. Stand quietly for at least one minute. As you inhale, feel as if clear water flows through your mind, carrying any thoughts or emotions with it, leaving in its place a quiet reflecting pool of water. As you exhale, release any tensions from your body and mind. You can also gaze in the pool of water and see any troubles, worries, or problems disappear in its smooth surface. Practice this exercise before you work with a dog.

This exercise frees trapped thoughts and builds conscious, deliberate awareness. In the beginning when you start practicing, thoughts leap out and grab your attention. You might think, "I forgot to pay the electric bill." Then, you remember that your air conditioner is twelve years old and less efficient, which is why your electric bill is higher. Before you know it, you are trapped! If your mind gets hooked, accept the thought and let it go. You can pay the electric bill later. The more you practice this exercise, the fewer thoughts will snare you.

Exercise 2: Feel Energy Between Your Hands

This exercise enables you to experience *chi*, the universal life energy.

Try this:

1. Stand or sit. Hold your hands in front of you twelve inches apart and shake them vigorously.
2. Bring your hands together so that your palms face each other. Hold your hands as close as possible without touching. Relax your fingers and your thumbs. Breathe.
3. Feel your heart beat in your chest.

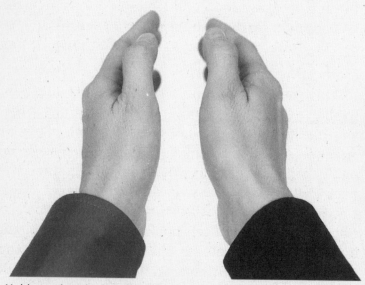

Hold your hands close together. LINDA BRUCE

4. Focus your attention on your fingertips and the palms of your hands. Feel how your hands pulse in rhythm with your heartbeat.

If you cannot feel your heartbeat, do not worry. Listening to your body is an acquired skill. With practice you will feel your heartbeat in your hands. However, realize that if you cannot feel your own heartbeat, it may be more difficult to feel a nonphysical energy between your hands.

5. After you feel your heartbeat in your hands, slowly separate your hands until they are twelve inches apart.

Separate your hands approximately twelve inches. LINDA BRUCE

6. Without rushing, bring your hands back together until they are one-half inch apart.
7. Repeat moving your hands together and pulling them apart slowly three times.
8. Next, increase the speed that your hands move until it seems like you are silently clapping. "Clap" at least five times.

What did you feel in the space between your hands? Some people describe it as taffy, magnets, pressure, tingling, heat, pinpoints of electricity, an accordion, a Nerf ball, or a cool breeze. What you feel depends on your sensitivity to the energy field. As your awareness increases, so will your ability to feel different aspects of energy.

Exercise 3: Build an Energy Field

This exercise shows you how to construct a protective energy field around you. If you cannot feel energy coursing through your body during this exercise, imagine that a clear silver liquid is moving through you.
Try this:

1. Separate your feet until the distance between your feet equals the width of your shoulders. Keep your feet parallel. Bend your knees slightly.
2. Bend over at the waist so that your arms hang loosely toward the ground. However, your hands do not need to touch the ground. Form an arc with your body to permit the earth's energy to enter your body.

Basic standing position.

LINDA BRUCE

Bend over at the waist.

LINDA BRUCE

3. Hold your hands as if you were going to grab a garden hose and pull it toward you. Move your right hand in a clockwise direction and your left hand counterclockwise. Your thumbs, which grip the inside of the "hose," rotate up to the top when your wrists turn to the outside.

4. As you rotate your hands simultaneously, inhale slowly while you "reach" into the earth for two roots of energy. Pull up the earth energy with your hands and bring it into the soles of your feet.

5. Slowly straighten your back, which draws up your hands and arms. Feel the earth energy rising through the soles of your feet, into your ankles, and up your calves, knees, and thighs.

6. When the earth energy reaches two inches below your belly button, face your palms out. Exhale.

7. Take another slow deep breath and let your hands rise to the sky. When your arms curve out over your head, approximately one and a half feet, feel for the sky's energy and "reach" for two clouds. Inhale while you pull the clouds toward you. Again, move your right hand in a clockwise direction and turn your left hand counterclockwise. Your thumbs, which are on the inside, rotate up to the top when you turn your wrists to the outside.

8. As you rotate your hands simultaneously, exhale, and pull the sky's energy down and into the palms of your hands.

9. Allow your hands and arms to drop slowly as

Raise your arms to the sky.

LINDA BRUCE

Place your right hand over your left hand. LINDA BRUCE

you pull the sky energy through your hands, wrists, forearms, elbows, upper arms, shoulders, chest, and abdomen.

10. When your hands reach your waist, place your right hand, palm up, on top of your left hand and breathe.

This exercise wraps you in a cocoon of earth and sky energy. This organic field protects you for approximately six to eight hours. Always create this invisible shield before you work with a dog so that your thoughts, moods, and emotions cannot affect your dog's well-being.

CHAPTER 9

THE ANIMAL ENERGETICS STRATEGY:

Five Techniques to Help You with Your Dog

Thick matted hair could not hide the sheltie's bony ribs as the stray dog limped into Susan's yard on three legs. Through the open kitchen window Susan watched as the sheltie circled underneath a tall pine tree and lowered her slender body against the thick carpet of needles. Quickly, Susan dried her hands and grabbed five dog treats from inside the blue ceramic jar next to the sink.

With quiet steps she approached the sheltie. Three feet from the dog Susan knelt down, called softly, "Puppy, puppy, puppy," whistled, and extended her flat hand with a dog biscuit. Wary eyes looked up and stared at the treat in Susan's hand. Susan stared at the ground in front of her feet, breathed deep and slow, and willed the dog to come. The sheltie did not move. Susan waited. Finally, the dog pulled herself up and hobbled toward Susan's outstretched hand.

Ten days later I met Susan's sheltie stray, Sammie, after Sammie snarled and snapped at Max, Susan's yellow Labrador. I will never forget seeing Sammie for the first time. She was curled into a fetal position on a corner of the living-room couch. A steady stream of spasms shook the dog's body; even her ears trembled.

Since our session would take place in the guest bedroom, Susan lifted Sammie from the couch and carried her to the room. Immediately, Sammie resumed her fetal position on the bed, her tail hiding her face as the tremors racked her body.

Resting on my knees, I leaned over and gently circled my arms around Sammie. With one hand I supported her back and hips, while my other hand used an Animal Energetics technique called a Soft Breeze to remove the fear and physical stress that caused Sammie's body spasms. Ten minutes passed. Fifteen. Sammie stopped trembling, picked up her head, and yawned. Simultaneously, she stretched out her front and back legs so that her soft white belly was exposed. Sammie sighed and the tremors vanished.

We waited. Five minutes turned into ten minutes, and the tremors did not return. Susan carried her back to the living room couch so Sammie could rest undisturbed during Max's session.

As soon as Susan called Max's name, he ran into the bedroom and jumped on the bed. Max had just lain down when we heard Sammie's feet running down the hallway. Sammie raced through the open bedroom door, jumped over Max, and slid next to him on the bed. Resting her back against Max, she stretched out her legs, closed her eyes, and fell asleep. During Max's entire session she never moved. In one Animal Energetics session Sammie changed from an insecure fear-biter to Max's friend.

The Animal Energetics system relieves tension, improves health, stimulates thinking, solves problems without pain, force, or stress, and produces happy dogs. It changes dogs' habitual physical, mental, and emotional responses by redirecting the energy flow, removing energy blocks, and balancing a dog's energy pattern. An Animal Energetics session involves touching a dog's body everywhere, since emotional, learning, and behavior problems reside in a dog's tight spots and untouchable places. Sensitive fingers, combined with a loving heart and a peaceful attitude, are all the Animal Energetics approach requires.

Recently, I met a sixteen-month-old rottweiler, J.R., whose aggressive tendencies were getting worse. In obedience class when the instructor tried to examine J.R. during the "stand for exam" exercise, the dog growled and snapped. (Stand for exam, a dog show requirement, involves a judge inspecting the dog visually and stroking the dog's head and back.)

During my first session with J.R., his handlers, Rob and Amy, told me that the current trainer, as well as strangers, could not touch the dog; even Rob could not touch J.R.'s legs. When dogs refuse or resent physical contact with a specific body part, it indicates a current or potential behavior, health, or learning problem. J.R. exhibited excessive growling, snapping, and lunging behaviors and rejected physical contact with most people. Before I could help Rob and Amy with J.R.'s show career, we needed to teach J.R. that physical contact was no cause for alarm. Instead, touching could bring him relief and satisfaction.

Most relationships begin with physical contact, and touching is basic. Dogs touch you with their noses or paws, and you touch them with your hands, feet, body, or lips. These interactions are important for the development of normal healthy relationships. Dogs who resist contact in specific body areas often display some type of problem or learning difficulty.

The five Animal Energetics techniques—Soft Breezes, Lakes, Mountains, Caves, and Rainbows—teach dogs that your hands bring them relief, comfort, and love.

Finding the Right Rhythm

Each Animal Energetics technique can be practiced with three different tempos—fast, medium, or slow. A dog's temperament determines which tempo you employ. During the same session, the tempo you use can change. You might start fast and end slow. As the dog's energy changes, so does your response.

A fast rhythm has a very quick beat: one-two, one-two, one-two, like a marching song. Use it with anxious and high-energy dogs to help them focus on you and to quickly release their nervous tensions. A medium rhythm keeps time like a waltz: one-two-three, one-two-three, one-two-three. Use this tempo when a dog is friendly or somewhat bouncy. A slow rhythm is like a lullaby. Its soft gentle presence does not scare a timid or frightened dog, but reassures the dog that no harm will come to him with its soothing presence.

Finding a Comfortable Position

During an Animal Energetics session you and your dog will probably change positions when you use the different techniques. Dogs can sit, lie down, or stand. You can kneel, sit on a chair, or lie next to the dog.

The dog's size and personality dictate his position during an Animal Energetics session. Small dogs like a Boston terrier, Chihuahua, or Lhasa apso can sit in your lap while you guide the dog's energy. Large dogs like Newfoundlands, Saint Bernards, or German shepherds can lie, sit, or stand next to you.

If you have an active dog, ask a friend to hold the dog while you practice. Your friend can place a hand or arm, depending on the size of the dog, under the dog's stomach while the other hand supports the dog's chest or neck. Turn to pages 162–166 to learn how to teach a dog to stand quietly.

One of the easiest positions for an Animal Energetics session when you work alone is to kneel down and form a V with your knees and thighs. With your knees on the ground, let your heels support your buttocks. Then, ask the dog to sit between your legs with his back next to your chest while his head faces out. This position allows

Have a friend hold your dog. JEFF CANTRELL

Basic Animal Energetics position. JEFF CANTRELL

you to keep an active dog contained between your legs, reassures a timid dog, and enables you to keep one hand on a dog's collar for control if necessary.

Three Hand Positions

There are three primary hand positions—two positions for your active hand and one position for your supporting hand. When you work with a dog, always keep two hands on the dog's body. The active hand directs energy, and the supporting hand receives it.

ACTIVE HAND POSITION #1

Place the pads of your index, middle, and ring fingers on the dog and rest the heel of your palm across from your fingers. Allow your thumb to rest on the dog's body. Your three middle fingers fit easily together, since they are next to each other and are about the same size. Use only the pads of your fingers and not the tips; long fingernails can dig into a dog's skin. Even soft fingertips can tear holes in a dog's energy field when used improperly.

Relax your little finger and thumb. If your fingers feel tight, shake the tension from your hands. Practice bending the knuckles and joints of your hands. Fingers stiffen when people concentrate and accidentally hold their breath. This tightens muscles and reduces your fingers' ability to contract or extend easily.

You want contact with, not pressure against, the dog's skin. Contact means your fingers rest on the dog's

Active hand position #1. LINDA BRUCE

fur, settle lightly against his skin, and connect with the energy inside the dog's body. When you move your fingers, the dog's skin also moves slightly. If your fingers skim over the fur, dogs feel as if tiny little flies are walking over their body, which irritates them. However, avoid using so much pressure that you actually displace the dog's muscles and cause discomfort. Instead, use sensitive fingers to make contact with the skin and direct the energy.

ACTIVE HAND POSITION #2

You can also use one finger or your thumb individually. When I work with a miniature schnauzer, three fingers will not fit comfortably on the dog's muzzle, so I use only one finger. Even with large dogs like Newfoundlands, I use one finger or my thumb when I direct the energy in their paws.

If your dog is aggressive or a fear biter, seek professional assistance before you try an Animal Energetics session.

Active hand position #2. JEFF CANTRELL

SUPPORTING HAND POSITION

Place your supporting hand so that your entire hand—palm, fingers, and thumb—rests against the dog's fur. Your supporting hand balances the energy generated by your active hand. Its presence keeps freshly stimulated energy from rushing through and out of the dog's body. When possible, rest your supporting hand on the opposite side of the dog's body across from your active hand.

The Relaxation Response

Reducing a dog's stress level is an important aspect of the Animal Energetics system. If a dog's body is tense, tight, or withdrawn, energy cannot circulate easily. Blocked energy retards learning, slows healing, and maintains bad behaviors. When a dog relaxes, energy flows smoothly. The following responses indicate that your dog is releasing inner tension: licking, sighing, snorting, drooping lower lip, breathing slower, breathing deeper, yawning, drooling, standing up and shaking, or stretching out both front and back legs.

If a Dog Is Injured

Do not begin an Animal Energetics session at cuts, bumps, wounds, bruises, or surgical incisions. Attend to a traumatized region last, since injured areas are ex-

Supporting hand position. JEFF CANTRELL

tremely sensitive. Before your hands pass near them, allow the energy you stimulate in other parts of a dog's body to flow to the injured area. At the end of a session, you can direct the energy at a particular site.

Animal Energetics Technique #1: Soft Breezes

When you think of a soft breeze, do not confuse it with a cold, harsh, north wind. Soft breezes go anywhere. They skirt around hills and valleys, lightly caressing everything they encounter. The Animal Energetics technique called the "Soft Breeze" assists energy in flowing smoothly throughout a dog's body. The Soft Breeze calms nervous energy, relieves pressure, cools hot areas, and connects one area of a dog's body to another area. Soft Breezes give dogs a new awareness of their bodies and balance their energies. As you glide along a dog's body, the energy you bring to the surface will follow your hands. Each pass draws the dog's excess, nervous, or painful energy out of the dog's body.

If you cannot touch a dog with a Soft Breeze in a sensitive area such as on the face, near the genitals, or on the paws, avoid those locations until the dog relaxes and learns that your touch brings him comfort and relief. Then, try a Soft Breeze in a sensitive site.

Since the purpose of the Soft Breeze is to connect and balance the dog, pass over all areas of a dog equally. For example, if you breeze down one front leg, glide down the other front leg. Always keep both hands on a dog to keep his energy in balance. Your active Soft

Soft Breeze on Trevor's ear. JEFF CANTRELL

Soft Breeze hand. LINDA BRUCE

Soft Breeze at Red's shoulder. LINDA BRUCE

Breeze hand presses lightly into the dog's fur, stimulating the dog's internal energy as it moves along his body. Your supporting hand rests on the opposite side of the dog's body when possible and receives the energy generated by the Soft Breeze. Don't stop when you reach the end of a dog's tail or ear but continue past the tip for two or three inches, drawing the energy out. Then, close your fingers against your palm and stabilize the energy by breathing deep and pausing.

When you apply Soft Breezes it does not matter if a dog stands up, lays down, or sits. Occasionally, you might ask the dog to change positions so you can reach a hidden paw or other body part.

Follow these steps:

To activate the energy in your hand, practice the feeling energy exercise on pages 172–74 or shake your hands, and while you rub them together, send feelings of love, warmth, and caring into the palms of your hands.

1. Rest your active hand on the dog's fur, and hold it at a 60-degree angle to the direction of your hand motion. Keep your fingers together and slightly bent, since separate fingers can tear tiny holes in a dog's energy field.
2. Rest your supporting hand on the dog.
3. Start at the dog's shoulder. Pass your active Soft Breeze hand in one smooth stroke from the dog's shoulder until you reach his rear end. Place your Soft Breeze hand on the dog's side below your previous position and move along the dog's

body. Repeat until you have covered the dog's entire side.

4. Run Soft Breezes down the other side of the dog's body.

5. Move your supporting hand near the dog's withers or ribs and slide Soft Breezes down each of the dog's front legs.

6. With your supporting hand near the dog's hips, run Soft Breezes down each of the dog's back legs.

7. It doesn't matter whether your dog's tail is short, curved, stubby, or long; slide your active hand along the dog's tail. Don't stop when your hand comes to the end of the tail. Continue until your hand stops approximately three inches past the tip of the tail.

8. After your last Soft Breeze, shake the unbalanced energy off your hands, place both hands on the dog's body, and stabilize the dog's energy by breathing deep and pausing.

APPLICATIONS

Soft Breezes bring a gentle state of relaxation and awareness to a dog's body. Use them to check a dog for potential physical or behavior problems, relieve summer heat and overexertion, reduce excess energy, calm excited dogs, help the energy stimulated by the other Animal Energetics techniques to flow into each other, and as a "Leaving Routine" to center your dog before you leave home.

Animal Energetics Technique #2: Lakes

Think of a dog's body as an unknown country covered with underground lakes. Lakes are pools of pressure that unreleased can explode as excessive barking, digging, licking, fear responses, and hyperactivity. Lakes exist in hidden places that affect dog minds and bodies. The Animal Energetics technique called "Lakes" allows you to tap into this subtle aquifer, release pressure, reduce stored up tensions, and change habitual responses.

Before you practice with your dog, picture a lake on a warm summer day. The water is blue, calm, and softly laps the shore. Allow this feeling of tranquility to enter your mind and hands. After you complete a few Lakes, if your hand starts feeling stiff take a break. Shake your hands, breathe deeply a few times, or practice the feeling energy exercise on pages 172–74. Tight hands stop the energy's movement and prevent a dog from responding as easily to your touch.

Lakes can be three inches across or one-half-inch across; their size depends on where they are located on a dog's body. Small Lakes fill ears, muzzles, and paws. Large Lakes occupy sides, hips, backs, and shoulders. Place enough Lakes to fill a specific area like a shoulder or a hip, but leave space between them. After you form individual Lakes, connect them to each other with a Soft Breeze. Since the purpose of Lakes is to relieve stress, if you cannot determine where your dog stores stress inside his body, apply them everywhere.

When you apply Lakes it does not matter whether a

dog stands up, lays down, or sits. Occasionally, you might ask the dog to change positions so you can reach a hidden paw or other body part.

During a master Animal Energetics session I cover a dog's body with Lakes. Five years ago when a husband and wife brought me their six-year-old shar-pei for a master Animal Energetics session, I experienced again the ability of Lakes to remove fear and replace it with trust.

In the beginning of the session the husband held the dog's collar when I started, since she had growled and lunged before at strangers. After twenty minutes the husband released his grip on the dog because she had not growled or snapped but remained quiet and attentive.

When I started forming Lakes on the dog's legs and paws I looked up and saw the husband and wife staring at each other with raised eyebrows, shaking their heads as I made tiny Lakes on the dog's paws. When I finished forming Lakes they told me the dog had never allowed anyone to touch her paws. In fact, their veterinarian tranquilized her in order to trim the dog's nails.

Her handlers learned during the Animal Energetics session that their dog was not instinctively aggressive. She was an intelligent, tense, anxious dog that could not release her inner tensions without assistance.

Follow these steps:

1. Rest your supporting hand on the dog's body.
2. Begin at the dog's shoulder. Inhale while your hand forms the Lake. With the pads of your active hand's fingers, follow the Lake's outer edge by moving in a clockwise direction:

- Start at the bottom, or south side, of the Lake.
- Next, curve west.
- Then, bend north.
- Finally, drop to the east and return to the south starting point.

Keep curving around the Lake until you reach the west side again. This completes the energy cycle. If you stop before you reach the Lake's western edge, a dog's energy becomes unbalanced, which increases anxieties, impedes the flow of energy, intensifies behavior problems, and impedes learning.

Lakes are not whirlpools. Make one circuit of a Lake. Do not go around and around in the same spot on a dog's body. When you repeat a Lake in the same place, you create energy holes, imbalances, or losses in a dog's energy field.

3. When you complete the Lake, exhale. Raise your fingers perpendicular to the dog's body—about three or four inches. Feel how your fingers draw the dog's energy with them as they rise.

4. Choose a nearby location and form another Lake. Repeat. You can form Lakes on paws, ears, muzzles, legs, necks, bodies, chests, hindquarters, or shoulders. To keep a dog in balance, if you form

Lakes. JEFF CANTRELL

Lakes on one side of a dog's body, also create Lakes in the same area on the other side.

5.. After you fill an area with Lakes, connect and smooth the energy between the Lakes by gliding over the same area with a Soft Breeze.

6. If a dog glances or moves away slightly from your touch in a specific area, avoid that location until the dog relaxes from the energy work in other places.

If your dog has an untouchable area, follow these steps:

- Begin in a place the dog enjoys and form several Lakes.
- Next, move your hand to the sensitive area and make one Lake very quickly.
- Immediately, return to an area the dog likes and form more Lakes.
- Repeat the previous steps.
- When a dog is comfortable with one Lake in a sensitive area, add two Lakes and return to the safe place to make more Lakes. Repeat slowly, increasing the number of Lakes in a sensitive area.

Working with sensitive areas can require more than one session, but once the dog learns your hands make him feel good, he will accept, relax, and enjoy the contact on formerly untouchable areas.

APPLICATIONS

Lakes release pressure and tension stored inside a dog's body. Use them to reduce digging, chewing, excess energy, puppy biting, mouthing, and fear responses to thunderstorms, people, and other animals. In addition, you can apply Lakes to decrease bruising, swelling, aching, sprains, stiffness, and congestion, as well as focus attention and improve breathing.

Animal Energetics Technique #3: Mountains

Mountains channel energy. In the same way hikers climb mountains to gain the summit, and then walk down bringing the mountain's energy with them, you can use your hands to raise and lower the energy present in a dog's legs. If you think of your hands as climbing the sides of a mountain, when you place them on a dog's leg you can awaken, shift, direct, and ground a dog's energy.

When I started training my dog, Red Sun Rising, for Agility, I realized once again the importance of the Animal Energetics technique called "Mountains." In Agility, where a dog places his feet determines if he maintains his balance or falls off an obstacle. In the case of the high Dog Walk, a misplaced foot causes a dog to fall over four feet to the ground. Dogs can become permanently disabled from a fall at this height.

The Dog Walk obstacle consists of one cross plank and two ramp planks, nine- to twelve-inches wide and twelve feet long, at least four feet off the ground. A dog races up the first ramp, runs the plank, and hurries down a second ramp in seconds. Small schnauzers run across this obstacle with room to spare. My golden retriever must narrow his stride and cross his legs to stay on the narrow boards. This is a difficult task for an exuberant sixteen-month-old dog who forgets where his feet are. When I move Mountains on his legs before we work out, they remind Red Sun Rising to pay attention to his legs and to place his paws carefully.

The best way to apply Mountains on a dog's leg is to stand a dog quietly in one spot; that way you can easily reach all four legs. If your dog does not know how to stand without moving, is injured, or arthritic, ask a friend to support him while he stands, or apply Mountains while he lies down.

Follow these steps:

1. Start at the top of the front leg, where the leg joins the body. Use two hands and place one hand on either side of the dog's leg and cover your left fingers with your right fingers. Position your hands parallel to the ground.

Large dogs, like mastiffs or Newfoundlands, require two hands to form a Mountain. With medium-sized dogs such as German shepherds or golden retrievers, you can use one or two hands, depending on your preference. Only one hand is needed with small dogs like toy poodles or Boston terriers.

2. Cup the dog's leg between your hand(s) until you feel his fur and skin moving when you lift your hands one quarter of an inch to the count of *one* one thousand, *two* one thousand, *three* one thou-

sand, *four* one thousand. Avoid pressing hard! Remember you are drawing energy up the dog's legs, not raising muscle mass. As you move the energy up with your hands, inhale. Feel how the energy rises up from the dog's foot to where your hands are located.

3. Pause four seconds. You will change the energy from rising to sinking when you start to lower your hands.

4. Exhale as you slowly lower your hands one quarter of an inch to the count of *one* one thousand, *two* one thousand, *three* one thousand, *four* one thousand. As you reach *three* one thousand, gently spread your hands apart about three or four inches away from the dog's leg. Feel the energy follow your hands as you draw them away from the dog's body. Check that your hands are parallel to each other and to the floor.

5. Pause and breathe. Your relaxed breathing and quiet mind balance the energy inside the dog's legs.

6. Place your hands on the dog's leg below your previous position. Repeat your Mountain trip. Continue to change the location of your hands until you reach the dog's paw.

7. With a Soft Breeze start at the top of the leg and stroke down to the dog's paw. Depending on the size of the dog, you can use one or two hands. When your hand reaches the paw, tap it lightly a few times with your fingers. This tapping draws the energy into the ground.

(Steps continued on page 208)

Mountains. JEFF CANTRELL

Mountains release. JEFF CANTRELL

8. Repeat the same Mountain journey for the other legs.

If you cannot form Mountains on all four legs, then do both front legs or back legs. Never form Mountains on just one leg, because it disturbs the dog's internal balance.

APPLICATIONS

Mountains focus a dog's attention on his feet. They free up energy residing in hips, shoulders, and backs, as well as improve a dog's gait. Mountains help with digging, jumping, excess energy, and leash pulling. In addition, use them to reduce swelling, stiffness, and sprains, and to release stored emotions.

Animal Energetics Technique #4: Caves

Dog mouths and muzzles are two of the most important body parts because dogs use them to inspect and interact with the world. Dogs nudge you with their noses for attention. They sniff clothes, furniture, leaves, and hands to discover where you have been, who has visited, or what is new. They lick, chew, or clamp their jaws when stressed.

The Animal Energetics technique called "Caves" recognizes that many dogs store tension, fear, and aggression inside their mouths, as well as the problems associated with teething and the setting of permanent teeth. Explore your dog's mouth when he is a young puppy, and it will decrease his need to bite, mouth, and chew.

When altering the energy patterns inside a dog's mouth, enter it like you would a cave. Caves are dark, unknown places where danger lurks or treasure hides. Sharp stalactites and stalagmites, called teeth, warn travelers to be cautious if they want to avoid feeling the unpleasant points that surround this opening. Explore carefully! You do not want to damage the delicate structures inside this hollow hill.

When one of my clients brought home Rocky, a Shiba Inu puppy, we started exploring his "Cave" when he was eight weeks old. Shibas are big dogs in small bodies. They are spirited, lively, and independent. Because they can be bold, they have been used for hunting game and guarding property.

Rocky's handler, Darla, said Rocky had a "wild dog routine." Rocky raced all over her house at top speed, nipping and biting Darla whenever she got close. His open mouth was always searching for her hand, arm, shirt, shoe, or pants leg.

During Rocky's first master Animal Energetics session, Caves, Lakes, and Soft Breezes changed a squirming, wiggly, biting puppy into a quiet canine. Within fifteen minutes of starting the session Rocky fell asleep, totally exhausted; his running, biting, and active energy all released. Daily Animal Energetics and special Cave sessions changed Darla's "wild dog" into a calmer puppy who no longer snatched at her with his mouth.

The first few times you explore your dog's mouth, he might raise his head or move around to avoid contact with your fingers. If the dog shifts, move with him.

Placing the dog in the basic Animal Energetics dog position described on page 183 uses the natural barriers of your legs and body to help the dog's mouth stay within easy reach. Once the dog understands how good Caves make his mouth feel, he will sit quietly for you.

Follow these steps:

1. Place your supporting hand next to the dog's neck, cheek, or muzzle. The size of the dog determines how much area your hand covers. Place your active hand opposite your supporting hand.
2. Lead with the palm of your active hand and use a Soft Breeze to stroke the outside of the dog's muzzle from nose to ear. Repeat.
3. Switch sides with your hands and repeat step two.
4. Before you place your hands inside a dog's mouth, dip them in a bowl of water to moisten them.
5. With your active wet hand, place your finger pads next to the dog's gums at the corner of his mouth. (The size of the dog's mouth determines the number of fingers you use. With a large dog you could use two or three fingers; with a small

Don't put a dry hand inside a dog's mouth. Your fingers will feel like sandpaper and cannot pass smoothly over the dog's gums.

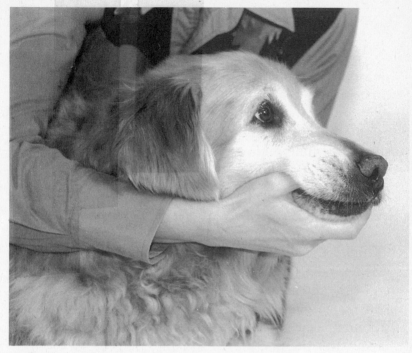

Caves. JEFF CANTRELL

dog you could use one finger or a thumb.) Use a Soft Breeze and glide your fingers across the dog's upper gum to the opposite corner. Repeat.

6. Change directions and send your active hand across the dog's gums again. Repeat.
7. Now use your thumb or fingers and slide across the dog's bottom gum. Repeat.
8. Change directions and pass your thumb across the gums again. Repeat.

APPLICATIONS

The Cave technique relieves stress and reduces the tension that assertive, excitable, or nervous dogs store in their mouths. Use it to decrease barking, chewing, teething, biting, mouthing, and fear responses, as well as to calm "take-charge" or high-energy dogs. It also stimulates gums and keeps them healthier.

Animal Energetics Technique #5: Rainbows

I met the German shepherd in October when she was fourteen and a half years old. She walked stiffly, and her tail was tucked between her legs. In fact, she had not wagged her tail in three years. Arthritis had stiffened her joints until walking and sitting were major tasks. After the first master Animal Energetics session, she wagged her tail. During the second session, she sat without discomfort. After the third session, all four legs moved independently when she walked. In March the dog died, but for six months she gained a new freedom and quality of life, as evidenced by her softly wagging tail.

Tails are rainbows. Their appearance lets you know what a dog is thinking and feeling. A tail that wags back and forth indicates a happy dog. Drooping tails show discomfort, pain, or submission. A stiffly held tail, with a rapid, staccato beat, identifies an angry dog. Whether a dog's tail is short, curved, stubby, or long, the tail completes a major energy pathway that starts at the dog's head and travels through his spine.

The Animal Energetics techniques called "Rainbows" assists energy in flowing smoothly through a dog's body. Before you create Rainbows, check to see if the dog is comfortable when you form Lakes on his rear cheeks and move Mountains on both back legs. Many dogs are sensitive about their hindquarters. If at any time a dog growls, his ears lie flat, or you see other signs of discomfort—stop! Do not continue. The dog must feel comfortable with your touch anywhere on his body before you turn his tail into a Rainbow.

Ask the dog to stand while you make a Rainbow with the dog's tail. If a dog cannot stand, the dog can lie down, or someone can support the dog while he stands. (See pages 162–66 to teach a dog how to stand.)

Follow these steps:

1. Begin by forming Lakes down the sides of both rear cheeks, under the tail, and on top of the tail.
2. With one hand pass a Soft Breeze down the tail. Do not stop when you come to the end of the tail, but let the energy follow your hand. When your hand is at least three inches past the tip of the tail, close your fingers against your palm, and stabilize the energy by breathing deep and pausing.
3. Move your supporting hand under the dock of the tail, so it props up the dog's tail where it joins the buttocks. Place your active hand on top of the tail, with enough space in between your hands so the tail curves and forms a Rainbow.
4. Gently move the base of the tail in a small circle to the right. Reverse and circle the tail to the left in a counterclockwise motion. When you finish,

Rainbows. JEFF CANTRELL

If the dog snaps, growls, or looks highly uncomfortable, stop what you are doing. Determine if the dog is in physical discomfort from your touch or if the dog is emotionally upset. In both cases, seek professional assistance.

complete the Rainbow by passing a Soft Breeze down the length of the tail.

If your dog has a short tail like a Scottish terrier, or a stubby tail like an Australian sheepdog, do not bend it into a Rainbow. If your dog has a curved tail like a Chinese pug, do not uncurl it. Use one hand and gently rotate the base of the tail.

APPLICATIONS

Rainbows release pressure and tension stored in a dog's hindquarters and spine. Increasing the energy flow between hips, legs, and spine helps dogs sit, walk, or stand with greater ease. In addition, Rainbows relieve stored emotions that cause dogs to be more assertive or afraid of events such as thunderstorms, strangers, or other animals.

The Five-Minute Session

`0:05`

In five minutes you can do a lot! You can relax muscles, release tight nerves, stimulate health, and change old habits. Once you learn the five Animal Energetics techniques, figure out different ways to use them with your dog. Use your imagination.

Change the area you focus on and combine different areas frequently. For example, one day move Mountains on all the dog's legs. Another day shape Lakes on the dog's shoulders and hips. The next day apply Lakes to both sides of the dog's spine and rear cheeks. Then, turn his tail into a Rainbow. Always end your sessions with Soft Breezes that cover the dog's body from head to toe.

Sandwich any problem spots in the middle of your session so that the energy you release in the beginning can start working on difficult areas before you ever touch them.

Work smarter not harder. Use additional Animal Energetics sessions to relax your dog and focus his attention before you begin your dog's schooling sessions. Conduct mini-sessions at any time during the day. For example, tap the dog's toes, glide a Soft Breeze over his body, form Lakes on his ears, or explore his Cave.

Incorporate Animal Energetics into your regular activities. Before I leave for an appointment, I practice the ten-second Leaving Routine. I pass Soft Breezes down Red Sun Rising's body and legs and tap his toes and nose. It's a great way to center this sixty-eight-pound ball of puppy energy so that he does not chew the rugs, destroy my couch pillows, or dig holes in my carpet.

Dogs eat shoes, dig holes in your backyard, and annoy neighbors with their barking when they are mentally, emotionally, or physically out of balance. The Animal Energetics approach allows you to redirect your dog's energy and create a healthy, happy companion.

CHAPTER **10**

SOLVE BEHAVIOR PROBLEMS USING bodyMIND AND ANIMAL ENERGETICS TECHNIQUES

Every dog is different, and every person is unique. In the end it's just you, your dog, and your relationship. No one can tell you what to do; you have to figure out what works in your situation. That is the truth. However, learning about different ideas and techniques can help you find the right answer for your particular situation. You cannot solve problems if you do not know what to do.

Your dog is not bad. The real problem is that you are missing the necessary ideas and techniques to easily change your dog's behavior.

This chapter details specific solutions to ten major dog behavior problems. It does not cover dog–dog aggression or dog–person aggression. Those problems require that you work directly with a professional.

The first day a dog enters your life, every interaction teaches him what you like and what you will accept. When you pet Dusty, the Newfoundland puppy, as she jumps to greet you, you teach her that jumping is an acceptable behavior. Of course, Dusty becomes confused when as an eighty-pound adolescent dog, she is punished for jumping.

Before you start working on your dog's problems, determine what role you have played in their development. Ask yourself what behaviors you and others have unintentionally encouraged, such as jumping, barking, or chewing on slippers. Most behaviors can be changed; however, it is important to understand the influence your husband, wife, children, friends, and neighbors have on your dog's behavior. Changing dog behavior requires that everyone works together toward the same result. For example, if you do not want Dusty to jump, your sixteen-year-old teenager cannot encourage Dusty to put her paws on his chest when he comes home after school every day.

Bad behavior does not appear instantly, but grows and develops over time. Frequently, what is cute as a puppy is unacceptable in an adult dog. Characteristics that are desirable when you live alone are not acceptable when you get married or have children.

A dog's behavior problem takes more than five minutes to develop, and it will probably require more than one session to solve. A simple rule to remember is that it takes thirty days to develop a new habit. Not thirty practice sessions in one day, but one practice session for thirty days in a row. If you work with your dog only once a week, realize that your dog's learning will progress more slowly.

Before you begin a teaching program, evaluate your dog's history. Review the following nine factors to determine how they might affect your dog's behavior and the successful resolution of any problems.

1. Age

Puppies must be introduced to everything. They must learn their name, where to defecate or urinate, how to fetch, how to bite gently and then not bite at all, how to relax, when to bark, and when to keep quiet. The list is endless. After they complete their puppy shots, they need to start socializing with other people and dogs.

Schooling sessions need to develop puppies' confidence and trust, as well as their ability to think their way through situations. Because puppies have short attention spans, lessons need to be focused and brief. Remember, puppies grow up. What is cute behavior for puppies may not be cute for forty-five-, seventy-five-, or hundred-pound adult dogs.

Adolescent dogs have the strength of adult dogs but still have puppy brains lurking inside their bodies. Depending on their previous training experiences they are either good listeners or have already learned to ignore their handlers. From approximately six to fifteen months, dogs become more independent, and even previously good listening skills can disappear. Do not get lulled by your puppy's good behavior; continue to work with your young dog as he grows up.

During adolescence, many dogs "forget" how to sit, down, stand, or come. Dogs often lose interest in their handlers and ignore them. If this happens with your dog, go back to the basics and teach your dog how to focus on you. Attract your dog's attention by doing the old lessons in new ways. For example, if your dog refuses to come, drop to the ground, rest on your knees, cover your head with your hands, and make strange noises, whimper, whine, laugh, or squeak a toy. The dog's natural curiosity will compel him to inspect this sudden change in your behavior. Doing the interesting as well as the unexpected maintains the dog's attention on you.

Dogs attain physical maturity around two years of age. Frequently, dogs at this stage are still determining who is the "top dog" in their group of canines and humans. If there is a leadership vacuum, adult dogs are eager to fill it. Small reminders that you are in charge can keep most problems from developing into major issues. In addition, be consistent. For example, if you make a rule such as no begging at the table, always follow it.

Older dogs may develop hearing, sight, stiffness, or incontinence problems. This is a special time in a dog's life and can require you to alter your schedule and adapt to the dog's needs.

2. Breed or Type of Dog

Stereotypes exist for a reason! Terriers like to dig and chase critters. Greyhounds love to run. Wolf mixes are independent. However, just because you have a cattle dog does not mean that he will herd or nip the heels of your friends, but there is an increased likelihood that he will follow the tradition of his breed.

When you design your teaching program, build on your dog's abilities. For example, use running as an "activity reward" after you have been working on quiet exercises such as down or stay with your greyhound. In addition, teach your greyhound to run with you while you bike. Every dog needs to have exercise and lessons that take into account his natural strengths.

The behavior of dogs can also be affected by whether they have been neutered or spayed. An intact male dog faces more distractions naturally, which fosters an independent nature. The heat cycle in a bitch increases the amount of daily care required, as well as invites unwelcome doggy visitors.

3. bodyMIND Attitude

Is your dog lonely, anxious, insecure, aggressive, territorial, bored, frustrated, high-energy, low-energy, fearful, exuberant, or playful? These are all factors you need to consider when looking for solutions. You must design sessions that direct a dog's energy, relieve his stress, and stimulate his thinking ability. Only then can you end a dog's reliance on instinctual habits such as chewing, digging, urinating, self-mutilating, or barking when anxious, and replace them with new behaviors such as finding and chewing on a Kong toy while he waits for you to come home, or digging in a specially designed digging area.

If you have not performed the exercises in chapter 3, try them before you attempt to change your dog's behavior. Knowing how your dog learns can speed the problem-solving process.

4. Socialization Skills

The number of people, animals, objects, and places a dog normally sees affects his behavior. Take a few minutes and jot down the number of new people and animals that your dog meets every week. Now, add the number of people or animals the dog sees on a regular basis. For example, if your dog barks uncontrollably during a UPS delivery, figure out how many times the dog encounters the UPS carrier. Try to remember if the experience was positive, negative, or neutral. Then, ask yourself if your dog reacts to any person in uniform such as a mail carrier, police officer, military person, or just the UPS carrier. If it turns out only UPS deliveries cause your dog to bark wildly, determine if your dog reacts to a specific person, to truck noises, or if this is a territorial issue. With just a little analysis, you can determine the specific trigger for a dog's behavior and design schooling sessions to reduce or eliminate it.

5. Amount of Daily Exercise

All dogs need exercise. The difference is that some dogs because of their personality or breeding must have physical exertion; inactivity creates problems. For example, border collies are bred to run a hundred miles in a day. They do not make good apartment dogs for that reason, unless they live with long-distance runners, joggers, or bicyclists who take them along. An easy way to solve behavior problems is to increase the number of play and work sessions as well as the amount of exercise your dog receives daily.

6. Behavior Pattern

Think about when the behavior first started and your response to it. Did you ignore or encourage it? Determine when the behavior occurs. Mornings? Evenings? Weekends? Before you leave for work? After you leave for work? Figure out how often the behavior has happened. Once? Three times? For days, months, or years? Behaviors that happen over a long period eventually become part of an established lifestyle and are much harder to change.

Once someone called and asked me if I could teach her dog to go outside to eliminate. Before I said yes, I asked the woman how long the dog had been urinating and defecating inside the house. When the woman replied sixteen years, I told her that trying to change the dog's behavior at this time was inadvisable. The time to change behavior is when it first appears—not six weeks, eight months, or sixteen years later.

7. Changes!

Any time an undesirable behavior appears, decide if anything is different. Frequently, a change has occurred, perhaps the birth of a new baby, the monthlong visit of relatives, a new friend of your son's who teases the dog, a move to a new house, different flowers in the garden, new carpeting in the living room, a new animal in the house, a son or daughter moving away or returning to live with you, nearby road or house construction, or even a new grandfather clock. All of these conditions can affect your dog's behavior. Once you know what triggers a change in your dog's behavior, you can design schooling sessions to minimize its effect.

8. Location- or Person-Dependent Behavior

Determine where and when the behavior occurs. For example, does the dog chew on the wooden kitchen-table leg when you are home, or does he chew on it when you are away? Does the dog bark at home as well as in the car, at a friend's house, or at the pet store, or is he quiet in a new place?

A dog's behavior often changes when the physical situation changes. When you design schooling sessions, change locations and increase the number of distractions, once the dog masters the exercise in the current environment.

If your absence triggers the dog's problem behaviors, use Animal Energetics, develop your dog's relaxation response, and build your dog's confidence and trust. In addition, ask a friend or family member to work with your dog when you are not home so the dog learns he can act appropriately in spite of your absence.

9. Nutrition and Diet

If your dog's behavior changes, review your dog's diet. Dogs can develop allergies to foods that change their behavior. You can feed the same dog food for months or years without any problems, until suddenly a dog develops a reaction that causes him to lick or scratch constantly. In addition, dogs can be stimulated by the presence of particular foods that increase their activity level, just like people who react to sugar or caffeine. The absence of certain vitamins or minerals can also affect a dog's health and behavior. Check with a veterinarian who specializes in nutrition and diet about your dog's food.

Before you work with your dog, keep in mind the following six behavior-solution principles:

1. Work with one problem at a time. Do not try to stop your dog from jumping, chewing, digging, and barking at the same time. Choose one behavior and work with it. Then, choose another behavior and work with it. What you will discover

is that as one behavior improves, other behaviors also improve.

2. Identify the real issue behind any behavior problem. Ask yourself, what does the dog find rewarding about a particular behavior? For example, if you have an Akita who likes to chase neighborhood cats, think about why this stimulates his brain, body, or instincts. Or does the dog view the activity as his job because he needs a replacement to satisfy his working requirements?

3. Incorporate a variety of approaches to change behavior. Use five-minute exercise, schooling, and Animal Energetics sessions to stimulate your dog's interest and increase his learning progress.

4. Look for the obvious solution. For example, if you pick up your clothes and put away your shoes, the dog cannot chew them. Childproof locks on the cupboard where the garbage can is stored prevents a dog from rummaging through the trash.

5. Increase the amount and type of exercise. Allowing a dog to run around in the backyard is not a substitute for the sustained cardiovascular physical exercise that occurs on five-, ten-, twenty-, thirty-, or sixty-minute walks or runs down streets, sidewalks, and in parks. Include a "work-time walk" as part of your outside exercise program. For a description of a work-time walk, see page 89.

   If you cannot walk your dog outside, put a leash on him, and take him on a work-time walk inside your living room, apartment hallways,

> If you can only do one thing with your dog, take him on a work-time walk every day, and watch his behavior improve.

basement, garage, or in your backyard. Increasing the amount and type of exercise solves most behavior problems when it is accompanied with carefully designed schooling sessions.

6. Keep behavior problems in perspective. Rank your dog's behavior problems on a one-to-three scale, where a ranking of one shows the problem is annoying, two indicates the problem is serious, and three means the problem is dangerous.

Your dog's barking will not wake the dead. Her digging will not cause your sidewalk to crumble into a hole. His excess energy can be channeled constructively. Jumping can be redirected. Do not lose sight of your dog's most important gifts to you: unconditional love, enthusiasm, friendship, and companionship.

Barking

PROBLEM IDENTIFICATION: The issue is not that dogs bark. We want dogs to bark in warning if a stranger jumps over a fence in our backyard, or while playing with us.

Barking becomes a problem when a dog cannot control when he barks or how long he barks.

KEY POINT: To recognize that dogs need to bark but also to recognize your need, and your neighbor's desire, for quiet. To realize your responsibility is to teach dogs when and how much barking is appropriate.

RANK YOUR DOG'S BARKING

1 = *Annoying.* The dog is quiet most of the time, but when something out of the ordinary happens, the dog barks a lot.

2 = *Serious.* The dog barks frequently throughout the day, and ignores any requests to stop barking.

3 = *Dangerous.* The dog no longer barks, but growls as a threat or warning. Seek help from a professional immediately.

TEACHING CONSIDERATIONS

1. Has anyone contributed to your dog's barking and further agitated him by asking "Who's at the door?" "Who's in the yard?" "What is that?" and encouraged the dog to bark when he hears sounds, cars, or people? If so, ask them to stop. They are making the dog's barking worse by their behavior.

2. If the dog barks, do you pick him up, pet him, give him a treat, or speak in a syrupy, soothing voice? These actions strengthen a dog's barking response. They do not diminish it.

STRATEGIES TO CHANGE BEHAVIOR

Dogs normally bark in response to a change in their environment. The sudden appearance of running cats and joggers, playing children, moving cars and bicycles, or ringing doorbells can trigger a dog's barking. You need to determine why your dog barks because that will tell you which of these solutions will work best for your particular situation. If your dog barks only when you are not home, ask your neighbors to keep track when the dog barks. For example, if the dog barks only when the garbage is picked up, plan schooling sessions during that time period to address this particular problem. If your neighbors cannot help you, plan on spending different times outside your house to determine what causes your dog to bark.

I want Trevor, my golden retriever, to bark when someone knocks on my door or pulls up in my driveway. I recognize his need to bark when a cat comes through our backyard. However, I expect Trevor to understand that there are limits to the number of barks he can make in a row. By applying consistently the three-bark rule (see Solution 1), both Trevor and I win. Trevor satisfies his need to bark and my house stays fairly quiet whether or not I am home.

If your dog has a high Mental Power Level, try this:

SOLUTION 1. Teach your dog to recognize the number of times he barks and to stop barking once he reaches a preestablished limit.

The three-bark rule works because it recognizes the dog's need to bark and your need for silence. The three-bark rule gives the dog the opportunity to make a choice. He can quit barking and earn praise and rewards, or he can keep barking and receive a redirection or reprimand.

When your dog barks, allow him to bark only three times in a row, then say "quiet," "enough," "silence"; any word you want. If the dog quits barking, reward him. If the dog does not quit barking, give him a redirection: Say "down." Frequently, dogs will not bark when they lay down. Or, say "sit." Many dogs will not bark when they sit.

If the dog does not quit barking, give him a reprimand. Say "stop" and squirt him on the nose with water. As soon as he stops barking, praise and reward him.

Once you determine what causes your dog to bark, design different teaching situations to change your dog's reaction. Set a specific time when a friend can ring your doorbell, call you on the phone, or ride past your house on a bicycle while you are at home with the dog. Then, practice the three-bark rule.

SOLUTION 2. Praise and reward your dog every time he does not bark in spite of reasons to bark. For example, if kids run across your yard and your dog quietly watches them out the window, reward your dog.

SOLUTION 3. Use the playSMART approach and make a game out of teaching your dog to bark on signal. Then, the dog will not bark unless your signal is present.

To teach a dog to bark on signal, think of an activity that causes your dog to bark automatically. For instance, Chance always barks when you hold a squeak toy six inches in front of his nose. Stand in front of Chance, squeak the toy, and when Chance barks, say "bark" or "speak" while he barks. Praise Chance and reward him with the toy or a dog biscuit. Repeat.

Once Chance understands you want him to bark, add a physical signal with your hand. A common bark signal is to hold your thumb and fingertips together so they form a cone. Then, open your hand quickly and allow your fingers to spread completely out. The movement of your hand attracts Chance's attention and focuses it on your hand. You can also hold a toy inside your hand and squeak it. When you open your hand, the dropped toy becomes Chance's reward for barking. Once Chance understands your hand signal with the toy, remove the toy from your hand and only use the hand signal. Practice these steps, reward, and repeat.

After Chance barks on signal, he can learn to be quiet on signal. First, ask Chance to bark. After he barks three times, say "quiet," "enough," or "silence" and practice the three-bark rule (Solution 1). Increase the time between Chance's silence and his reward. Over time, many dogs refuse to bark unless they see the "bark" signal.

If your dog has a high Physical Activity Level, try this:

SOLUTION 4. Play calming music or talk radio to cover outside noises for your sound-sensitive dog.

SOLUTION 5. Close the drapes, curtains, or blinds so the movement- or sight-sensitive dog cannot see what happens outside the house. If you do not want to shutter the entire house, keep the dog in a room that can be sheltered from distractions while you are away.

SOLUTION 6. Change the dog from being an outside dog to an inside dog when you are gone. If you are worried about chewing or house soiling while you are away, turn to pages 238 and 258.

If your dog has a high Emotional Response Level, try this:

SOLUTION 7. Practice a five-minute Animal Energetics session at least once a day in order to develop your dog's relaxation response.

SOLUTION 8. Barking dogs frequently store stress in their mouths. Do at least three 10-second Cave sessions every day, and de-stress your dog's mouth. For the Cave technique turn to pages 208–12.

SOLUTION 9. Before you leave the house, use Soft Breezes and perform the ten-second Leaving Routine to decrease your dog's anxieties. Turn to page 216 for a description of the Leaving Routine.

Biting

PROBLEM IDENTIFICATION: The issue is not that dogs use their teeth to eat, chew, or destroy appropriate items. The problem is the handler has not taught the dog that biting people in any manner, shape, or form is forbidden.

KEY POINT: To recognize that a dog's primary mode of

contact is through his mouth, and to realize your responsibility to teach him acceptable ways and places for contact.

RANK YOUR DOG'S BITING

1 = *Annoying.* The puppy nips at your hands, shoes, clothes, or any part of your body he can reach.

2 = *Serious.* The young dog nips, tugs, and pulls at your hand, shoes, clothes, or any part of your body that he can reach.

3 = *Dangerous.* The adult dog has bitten you and punctured your skin. He may or may not have already bitten someone else.

TEACHING CONSIDERATIONS

1. How old is the dog? Puppies bite constantly to learn the strength of their jaws. Adolescent dogs bite to set their teeth. Your task is to teach puppies to recognize the power of their jaws and to bite softly. Then, you can teach them never to bite.

2. How many toys, rawhides, or bones are available for your dog to chew? Dogs need a safe outlet for their mouths. Direct the puppy or dog's desire to bite to appropriate toys, bones, or rawhides.

3. Have you or someone in your house agitated your dog by teasing, taunting, or playing roughly with him? Treat your dog in a gentle fashion and check his environment so that strangers cannot bother him. Do not allow anyone to tease the dog

by pulling or tugging on his ears, tail, or legs. Avoid playing with the dog so roughly that he thinks biting is part of a game. If you leave the dog outside when you are not home, check that your fence is solid and prevents anyone from taunting the dog through the fence.

4. Do you have a herding dog that was bred to nip cattle or sheep to keep them moving? Herding dogs with strong instincts often nip at people's heels when they do not have any animals to "work."

STRATEGIES TO CHANGE BEHAVIOR

We want puppies to bite! Then, we can teach them to control how often and how hard they bite. Puppies are not born with educated mouths. They must learn to control their jaws. It is your job to start teaching your seven- or eight-week-old puppy the rules of contact. By the time your puppy grows into an adolescent dog with

Never hit a dog to force him to stop biting. It can turn a simple biting problem into aggression. If your puppy or adolescent dog growls when you take toys away or when you correct him, seek professional help immediately. Also, turn to professionals if you have an adult dog who threatens to bite or who has bitten someone already. Adult dogs should not bite people for any reason. Aggression is a problem that requires expert handling.

permanent teeth, your teaching job should be completed. This gives you ten to twelve weeks to teach your puppy bite inhibition if you start working with your puppy immediately. By the time the puppy's adult teeth come in, all contact with your skin or clothes should be over.

Your first task is to teach puppies to bite softly. Then you can teach them not to mouth you at all. The difference between biting, mouthing, and aggression is one of intent. Puppies bite to develop and test the strength of their jaw muscles and their status. Adult dogs bite in reaction to specific events. For example, someone grabs the dog when asleep. The dog wakes up instantly and bites the person's hand. Many people cause their dogs to bite. Yet I know pit bulls with delightfully soft mouths, cattle dogs who do not nip at their family's heels, and retrievers who can carry a live bird in their mouths without injuring it. These dogs have one thing in common: They have been taught bite inhibition.

If your puppy or adolescent dog has a high Mental Power Level, try this:

SOLUTION 1. Yell "OUCH!" when puppy's teeth contact your skin, no matter how hard or soft the bite is. Use a voice that is not high-pitched and sharp, but lower than your normal voice. Squeaky, sharp sounds excite dogs. Turn away from your puppy or leave the room where he is. Ignore him for at least thirty seconds.

SOLUTION 2. Teach your puppy or dog how to recognize the correct items for chewing and biting. Praise him anytime you see him chewing on an acceptable object.

Turn to pages 238–45 to learn how to teach your dog the difference between acceptable and unacceptable items. In addition, direct your puppy's need to chew toward toys, balls, bones, or Kongs. See page 243 to learn how to stuff a Kong.

SOLUTION 3. Teach your puppy or dog the meaning of the signal "leave it." Practice the following steps:

Step 1. Hold a food treat that the dog likes in the palm of your hand. Tell the dog "take it," and let him eat the treat.

Step 2. Hold a second food treat in your hand. When the dog comes up to sniff or eat it, say "leave it" and fold your fingers over the treat. If the dog sniffs or bites your hand say "OUCH!" If the dog backs up or stops sniffing, praise him. Then, redirect to an appropriate item to chew. For example, ask him to "go find his toy/stuffed Kong/rawhide."

Step 3. Repeat this sequence a few times every day until your dog learns the meaning of the words "take it" and "leave it."

HELP
If the dog keeps biting or sniffing, repeat "leave it" and "OUCH!" If the dog ignores your voice, squirt him with water on his nose. Then, praise and redirect him.

If your puppy or dog has a high Physical Activity Level, try this:

SOLUTION 4. Change toys on a regular basis for your sight- or smell-sensitive dog. Remove a few of your dog's toys every week, hide them, and then put them out the following week. That way your dog always has something "new" to chew. Have inside as well as outside toys.

SOLUTION 5. Teething puppies and adolescent dogs frequently have sore gums. Give a touch-sensitive puppy a frozen washcloth or ice cubes to ease the pain.

If your puppy or dog has a high Emotional Response Level, try this:

SOLUTION 6. Practice a five-minute Animal Energetics session at least once a day to develop your dog's relaxation response.

SOLUTION 7. Do at least three 10-second Cave sessions every day to relieve his physical stress due to sore gums. To review the Cave technique turn to pages 208–12.

Chewing

PROBLEM IDENTIFICATION: The issue is not that dogs chew. We want dogs to build strong teeth, gums, and bodies by chewing rawhides, toys, treats, and eating their meals. Chewing becomes a problem when dogs chew inappropriate articles or destroy specific items.

KEY POINT: To recognize a dog's need to chew and to

recognize your responsibility is to provide appropriate directions and chew toys.

RANK YOUR DOG'S CHEWING

1 = *Annoying.* The dog occasionally chews on something he should avoid.
2 = *Serious.* The dog chews on anything within his reach.
3 = *Dangerous.* The dog destroys doorjams, window ledges, wooden blinds, or other personal or household items and appears to go into a "chewing frenzy."

TEACHING CONSIDERATIONS

1. Have you contributed to your dog's chewing problem by leaving your dog alone for long periods of time with nothing to do? Dogs need consistent attention, exercise, and schooling.
2. When you leave the house are you in a hurry, tense, or anxious? Do you excite your dog with play or an emotional good-bye that emphasizes the dog's isolation when you leave? Often, dogs chew to relieve nervous tension, and abrupt, chaotic, and speedy or emotional departures can unsettle dogs.
3. How old is the dog? Puppies chew when teething. Older dogs from the ages of six to twelve months, chew to set their permanent teeth.
4. Do you have a bitch in heat? Chewing is not shredding. Female dogs will shred paper, carpets,

or furniture to satisfy their nesting instincts. They may want to build a den even when they are not pregnant.

STRATEGIES TO CHANGE BEHAVIOR

Dogs are social animals who investigate the area they live in to find mental and physical stimulation. When dogs are left alone or isolated, they search for sensations to satisfy their need for contact, exercise, and food.

Dogs chew because it provides an outlet for teething, anxiety, boredom, loneliness, and frustration. In addition, chewing is self-rewarding as well as fun. Leather shoes get softer as they are chewed, shredded couches make wonderful nests or dens, and munching plants or stripping bushes satisfies instinctive urges. Knowing why your dog chews will help you determine which of these solutions will work best for your particular situation.

If you come home and discover that your dog has destroyed a favorite item, do not yell at your dog. Yelling or hitting will not teach the dog how you expect him to behave in your absence. Instead, find a different outlet for your anger. Determine what you need to teach the dog in order to prevent the destruction from happening again.

If your dog has a high Mental Power Level, try this:

SOLUTION 1. Use the playSMART approach and teach your dog the "find-the-toy" game.

Step 1. Find something that the dog likes to chew and play with that item and the dog.

Step 2. Place the toy on the floor near the dog and say "Find the toy!"

Step 3. When the dog picks up the toy, praise him.

Step 4. Use your body language to ask the dog to bring you the toy. For example, act excited, back up a few steps, and crouch down.

Step 5. Play with him.

Step 6. Place the toy farther away each time.

Step 7. Once the dog understands the find-the-toy game, ask the dog to wait while you hide the toy. Choose easy locations at first and then make them more difficult.

Once your dog plays the find-the-toy game, upon entering the house, *before* you touch or fuss over the dog say, "Find your toy." As soon as the dog brings you the toy, reward him and play with him. Dogs learn quite readily that you want to be met at the door with a toy in their mouths. Asking the dog to greet you with

HELP
If the dog just stands there uncertain and waiting, go to his favorite item, squeak it, or wave it in front of his nose. Get the dog to take it from you and chew on it. Praise him.

a toy often channels his anticipation anxiety into searching for the toy. In all probability, the dog will chew on the toy while he waits for you to come home.

SOLUTION 2. Teach your dog the difference between acceptable and unacceptable items to chew. Then, he can make choices based on previous schooling sessions.

Step 1. Set out a variety of toys, bones, and balls in a room and see which ones your dog plays with on his own. When he picks different ones up and chews them, praise him. Now you know which items are his favorite "chewies."

Step 2. Place two items on the floor in a room with the dog. One item is a favorite chew toy. The other, item X, is a previously chewed article, a new shoe, an unplugged electrical cord, or any item you want to teach the dog not to chew.

Step 3. If the dog chews on his favorite toy, praise him. If he sniffs or licks item X, say "leave it!" As soon as he stops sniffing or licking, redirect him. Say "Good boy. Go find your toy." If he gets his toy, praise him lavishly.

Repeat this session in different rooms of the house or outside in the yard over a series of days. Keep the teaching sessions short. Set up the situation and *wait* for your dog to make a decision. Be prepared to wait several minutes. Once the dog acts, respond to the dog's decision immediately with praise or a redirection.

SOLUTION 3. Praise and reward your dog every time you see him chewing on an acceptable item.

If your dog has a high Physical Activity Level, try this:

SOLUTION 4. Use the playSMART approach and teach your dog the "search" game so that he will have something to do when you are not home. The search game is the same as the find-the-toy game except there is more than one item for the dog to find or "search" for. For example, give the dog one "chewy" (a stuffed Kong or bone, rawhide, etc.) as you leave, and place other "chewies" in different locations throughout the house. Dogs learn quickly to search, find, and chew. One of my clients leaves three Kongs stuffed with her dog's breakfast throughout the house every morning. She prevents the dog's destructive chewing as soon as she leaves by focusing his efforts on finding his "chewies," which instantly rewards him with breakfast for chewing them.

SOLUTION 5. Supervise "take-charge" or high-energy dogs when you are home. Do not allow your new puppy or untrained dog to wander through the house unattended. For example, bring the dog and dog toys into your family room while you watch television and close the door.

Limit the area your dog has to roam in the house while you are gone to a single room such as a kitchen,

---

HELP
Stuffing a bone or Kong involves placing or wedging small, bite-sized pieces of food inside it so that dogs will chew, lick, and worry it until the food is gone.

utility room, or family room. Dogproof the space as much as possible. For example, put childproof latches on the cupboards, do not leave food sitting out on counters, and remove any electrical cords or other potential chewables.

SOLUTION 6. Hire a pet-sitter or ask a friend to take your dog on a work-time walk if you will be gone for eight hours or more. For additional information about work-time walks, turn to page 89.

SOLUTION 7. With sight- or smell-sensitive dogs, pick up your clothes, put away your shoes, close bedroom doors, put childproof locks on cupboards and closets, secure the lid on the trash can, build a fence around your prize flower garden, and have plenty of toys like Kongs, rawhides, bones, woolies, or squeakers for your dog to play with.

SOLUTION 8. Change toys on a regular basis. Remove a few of your dog's toys every week, hide them, and then put them out the following week. That way your dog always has something new to play with. Have inside as well as outside toys.

SOLUTION 9. Give touch-sensitive puppies a frozen washcloth or ice cubes to ease the pain of swollen gums.

SOLUTION 10. If your taste-sensitive dog has already chewed a table leg or a couch cushion in your absence spray Bitter Apple or a foul-tasting mouthwash on it. Or, rub some hot sauce on the chewed surface. If the dog chews it again, the taste will repel him.

SOLUTION 11. If your dog chews something that cannot be sprayed with a repellent, "booby-trap" the item.

To booby-trap something take clean, empty pop cans; place ten small, round stones in them; tape the cans shut; and tape a string from the cans to the counter, ledge, or surface's edge. That way if the cans are disrupted, they will fall down, bang along the side of the object, and interrupt the dog. For example, if your dog eats toilet paper rolls, rest two cans on top of the toilet paper roll. Tape the strings to the counter's edge so that when the dog pulls on the toilet paper roll, the cans fall down, startle him, and stop him from chewing. DO NOT BOOBY-TRAP YOUR WHOLE HOUSE! Work on one problem area at a time.

If your dog has a high Emotional Response Level, try this:

SOLUTION 12. Practice a five-minute Animal Energetics session at least once a day to develop your dog's relaxation response.

SOLUTION 13. Chewing dogs frequently store stress in their mouths. Do at least three 10-second Cave sessions every day, and de-stress your dog's mouth. For the Cave technique turn to pages 208–12.

SOLUTION 14. Before you leave the house, use Soft Breezes and perform the ten-second Leaving Routine to decrease your dog's anxieties. Turn to page 216 for a description of the Leaving Routine.

Digging

PROBLEM IDENTIFICATION: The issue is not that dogs dig. Dogs dig to bury bones, find other animals, locate good smells, create dens, cool off in hot weather or find shelter in cold weather. Digging becomes a problem when dogs dig in an inappropriate area and destroy something you value.

KEY POINT: To recognize that dogs need to dig and to recognize your desire for a yard or house that does not look like a moonscape. To realize that your responsibility is to channel your dog's desire to dig into appropriate areas.

RANK YOUR DOG'S DIGGING

1 = *Annoying.* The dog occasionally digs a few holes.
2 = *Serious.* The dog frequently digs large holes in areas where they should not be located.
3 = *Dangerous.* The dog digs huge craters and in the process destroys large sections of the yard or carpeting.

TEACHING CONSIDERATIONS

1. Are you providing appropriate shelter for your dog? Is the dog digging to find relief from the sun, rain, or snow? Dogs must have protection from the heat or cold. It is only natural that your dog digs if you have not provided him with appropriate shelter.
2. Is the dog bored or looking for an escape route? Dogs often dig when they are underexercised and understimulated in their current surroundings, or to release frustration.

3. Is the dog a terrier type, bred to dig after small animals? Over the years some breeds have been bred selectively to develop their digging ability.
4. Is the dog hungry or does the dog have a vitamin or mineral imbalance that causes him to eat roots, vegetables, grass, or dirt? Check with a veterinarian who specializes in nutrition to determine if this is your dog's problem.

STRATEGIES TO CHANGE BEHAVIOR

This is how digging happens. Lonely dogs and dogs with excess energy who have been isolated and understimulated for too long excavate mounds of dirt to bury food, eat roots, find small animals, escape a boring yard or kennel run, and create shelter from the heat, rain, or cold. Digging provides immediate rewards for dogs. For example, the fresh scents in the ground reinforce dogs' desire to dig. When dogs escape, they can explore the attractions on the other side of the fence. If dogs uncover a bone, they eat it. When they find a small animal, they chase it. Learning why your dog digs will help you determine which of the following solutions will work best for your particular situation.

Some dogs have a very strong need to dig, and it is important to accept this fact. Find a place in your yard where digging is not only allowed but encouraged. Digging is a natural dog behavior. The best solutions direct dogs' digging to appropriate places and provide enough stimulation for them so that they do not dig out of boredom, frustration, or loneliness.

If your dog has a high Mental
Power Level, try this:

SOLUTION 1. Teach your dog to recognize a specific location where digging is permitted.

Create a digging area (approximately four feet by four feet) with chew toys, bones, balls, or food treats hidden in the dirt. Mixing sand or peat with the dirt can make it easier for you to hide items in the digging area. If possible, choose as the dog's digging area a space where the dog likes to dig.

To teach your dog to dig in a specific area have him watch you bury a yummy food treat in the digging area. Then, cover it up. Tell the dog to dig for the bone or find the treasure. Praise the dog when he finds it. Eating the treat provides him with an instant reward for digging. Repeat this hiding and digging treat activity for a few days. Soon, the dog will search the digging area for treasures. Now, hide more treats, bones, balls, or branches inside the area. Whenever you see the dog digging there, praise him. In the beginning, seed the digging area with buried treasure every day.

You can also create a digging box inside the house—in a laundry room, basement, attic, or garage—with plywood, four-by-fours, and small pebbles.

SOLUTION 2. If a dog digs because he needs a cool area, create a shady cover with a tarp, buy a doghouse, purchase a child's swimming pool, plant bushes and trees, or install a misting system. If a dog digs because he needs a burrow or a den, create one with a doghouse, blankets, and straw.

If your dog has a high Physical Activity Level, try this:

SOLUTION 3. Let a high-energy dog outside only if you can supervise him. Praise the dog when you see him chew on a toy or lie in the sun. If the dog starts to dig, redirect him. Ask him to go find a toy, or send him to the digging area.

HELP
If the dog does not respond, say "stop!" Squirt him with a long-range water gun as he digs. Praise him as soon as he stops digging. Then, redirect him.

SOLUTION 4. Put a fence around the area where you do not want the dog to dig, for example, around your flower or vegetable garden.

SOLUTION 5. To prevent digging in an area where a sound-sensitive dog currently digs, place inflated balloons inside a hole and cover them up with a light coating of dirt so that when the dog starts to dig they pop.

SOLUTION 6. To prevent digging in an area where a smell-sensitive dog currently digs, put some cayenne pepper or dog feces in the hole. When the dog goes to dig there, pepper will cause him to sneeze and back away, and he will avoid digging through his feces.

If your dog has a high Emotional
Response Level, try this:

SOLUTION 7. Digging dogs frequently store stress in their paws, legs, and rear end. During your daily five-minute Animal Energetics session, form Mountains on the dog's legs and Lakes on his paws and rear end. Make sure you turn his tail into a Rainbow. For the Mountain, Lake, and Rainbow techniques turn to chapter 9.

SOLUTION 8. Digging dogs also store tension in their mouths. Do at least three 10-second Cave sessions every day, and de-stress your dog's mouth. For the Cave technique turn to pages 208–12.

SOLUTION 9. Before you leave home, use Soft Breezes and perform the ten-second Leaving Routine to decrease your dog's anxieties. Turn to pages 216 for a description of the Leaving Routine.

Fear Responses to Noise, Thunderstorms, People, Objects, and Other Animals

PROBLEM IDENTIFICATION: The issue is not that dogs are timid, apprehensive, unconfident, or fearful. The issue is that the dog's fear response negatively impacts your lifestyle and causes you to worry about his mental stability and physical well-being. The problem is the dog lacks inner quiet and has not learned a relaxation response.

KEY POINT: To recognize that how dogs mentally and emotionally feel affect their behavior. To realize that your responsibility is to find ways to increase your dog's coping abilities.

RANK YOUR DOG'S FEAR RESPONSE

1 = *Annoying*. The dog acts normally most of the time, but when something out of the ordinary happens, the dog becomes frightened.

2 = *Serious*. The dog acts nervous all the time, trembles and shakes during normal occurrences, and when the unusual happens becomes frantic.

3 = *Dangerous*. The dog takes every behavior to its extreme. For example, fear has caused the dog to destroy window ledges, doorjams, and wooden shutters, suffer from constant diarrhea, race frantically through the house, or bark nonstop.

TEACHING CONSIDERATIONS

1. Did you provide a continual variety of socialization experiences for the dog while he was growing up? Exposure to different people, places, and things teaches dogs healthy and friendly ways to respond and interact.

2. Did you increase the amount of attention and reassurance the dog received when he ran away, hid, trembled, or cowered? These actions strengthen a dog's fear response. They do not diminish it.

3. Did anyone tease the dog, shoo him away with a broom, or shoot him with a slingshot or BB gun? Did the dog ever get his tail or paws run over by a wheelchair, stroller, tricycle, or bike? Did trash cans, boxes, or other objects fall on the dog unex-

pectedly? Was the dog ever repeatedly hit, beaten, or terrorized? These actions trigger and deepen fear responses. Whenever children or adults play with your dog, make sure that all the games are not tug, pull, run, and chase, but include quiet times and friendly rubs. Remember, children and dogs should always be supervised whenever they are together.

4. What type of contact do you have with the dog? Are you always touching or holding the dog? Does the dog get upset if he cannot be near you? Excessive touching or constant contact often creates a person-dependent dog and inhibits the dog's confidence to handle events when left alone.

STRATEGIES TO CHANGE BEHAVIOR

The handler plays an important role with dogs who react with fear. If puppies are exposed to traumatic events, those experiences can be difficult to erase in an adult dog. However, when puppies meet nice people and children, friendly, well-behaved animals, and learn that new objects and places mean more fun and games, it prevents serious fear responses from developing.

When dogs are teased by children or adults, or shooed away with brooms or vacuums, it teaches dogs to be afraid of people or moving objects. In addition, when dogs are repeatedly hit or beaten, they quickly learn to fear and avoid whoever or whatever struck them. Even when an object accidentally falls on dogs, it can provoke fear responses to canes, crutches, boxes, or children's toys.

Fear comes in many forms. Pounding hearts and muscle twitches often transform into violent tremors that shake entire dog bodies. In extreme cases dogs "freeze" and black out. When dogs feel trapped, they might attack the threatening person or object in order to escape. Dogs howl, bark, hide, tremble, vomit, attack, or run away when they are afraid.

Your reaction to their display of fear can increase or diminish it. If you speak softly, pet, and hold dogs to reassure them, your attention strengthens instead of diminishes their fear response. In addition, it teaches dogs that safety exists only in your presence. This develops dogs who want to touch or be near their handlers at all times. When their handlers are not present, they become more frantic and uncontrollable. Over time, dog fear responses grow more intense if someone does not intervene in ways that build their confidence, rather than dependence, on their handlers. Dogs cannot lose their fears without assistance, since their fear results from mental and emotional distress.

Many of the traditional methods of dog handling have little effect with dogs who exhibit fear responses. For example, heeling on a leash does not teach a dog to be unafraid of thunderstorms. Learning how to sit or down does not teach a dog to ignore the ringing of a telephone and the chugging of a lawnmower or vacuum.

Physically relaxed and mentally calm dogs can face loud noises, frightening objects, and strangers without cycling back into fear responses. An effective method for increasing dogs' confidence is Animal Energetics. Animal Energetics significantly relaxes dogs and decreases their sensitivity to noise, thunderstorms, people, objects, and other animals. Do not confuse Animal Energetics with petting or rubbing to comfort your dog. Animal Energetics is a process that relieves physical, mental, and emotional stress by developing dogs' relaxation responses. Turn to chapters 8 and 9 for a thorough discussion of Animal Energetics principles and practices.

You will discover that as your dog gets braver in one situation, his confidence in other areas builds. Your challenge is to have patience. Your dog did not develop his fears overnight. It will take time and the creation of special learning situations to develop your dog's ability to stay calm, quiet, and centered in the presence of potentially frightening situations.

If your dog has a high Mental Power Level, try this:

SOLUTION 1. When you are at home, use the playSMART approach and make a game out of teaching your dog to approach people or objects. Ask your dog to follow a trail of treats to an object or person. The most tempting treat is placed in the scariest location, for example, on top of a vacuum or next to a visitor.

SOLUTION 2. If you are on a walk and your dog is scared

Do not force your dog to confront a situation. A dog who feels trapped might fight or bite.

HELP

If your dog becomes afraid, do not tighten your grip on the leash. A taut leash telegraphs your apprehension to the dog and increases his apprehension. Instead, teach your dog to walk with a relaxed leash. (A relaxed leash has "give" or "droop" in the line.) When confronted with a difficult situation, stay calm and act happy.

Redirect your dog's attention to you. Walk in a different direction, and ask the dog to sit, down, twist, back up, shake hands, roll over, or any other behavior he knows.

of people, when you meet and talk with someone, stand next to the person and not across from him. Let the dog figure out from your body language that this is not a threatening situation.

Do not force the dog to go up to any person! Let the dog decide if he wants to greet someone. If the dog chooses to come close, ask the person not to reach down and pat the dog on the head. Later on, the person can hold out his hand for the dog to sniff.

If you plan this "meeting" in advance, the person who holds out his hand can have the dog's favorite food treat in his hand. If every person the dog meets allows the dog to approach, then rewards that greeting with food, the dog learns that strangers are really friends he has met for the first time.

If your dog has a high Physical Activity Level, try this:

SOLUTION 3. When you are away from home, close drapes, curtains, or blinds so there are fewer visual disruptions for your sight-sensitive dog.

SOLUTION 4. When you are on a walk, ask different friends and their *well-behaved* and friendly dogs to meet you in a neutral location like a park and go on a walk with you and your dog.

SOLUTION 5. At home, play music or talk radio to cover outside noises for your sound-sensitive dog.

SOLUTION 6. Associate noise with pleasant events. For example, if your dog is afraid of noise, play dinnertime noise games. Tap his bowl or the can of dog food with a spoon. Make that a signal that dinner is coming. Start out softly, but eventually increase the volume and add new sounds. Make noise when you play with your dog. For example, start by laughing and talking and build until you can shriek with delight, whoop, or shout when you play with your dog.

If you want to socialize your dog with other dogs, seek professional assistance. For example, bring a shy puppy to a puppy kindergarten class.

If your dog has a high Emotional
Response Level, try this:

SOLUTION 7. Improve your dog's relaxation response by practicing Animal Energetics for five minutes every day. Incorporate as many daily five-minute sessions as your schedule allows.

Create a "safe area" where you practice Animal Energetics. Place towels, blankets, or a dog bed in a large closet, in a corner of the family room, under a counter, or behind a couch. A safe area gives the dog a place to go where he can feel secure even when you are not home.

In the beginning, practice Animal Energetics during nonstressful times. Once you can touch your dog, and he releases his tension through yawning, short puff breaths, a quick body shake, full-body stretches, lies down, closes his eyes, and breathes deeper, you are ready to practice Animal Energetics during an event that normally triggers the dog's fear response.

Start with a situation that causes the least amount of stress in the dog. For example, if the dog reacts to objects like a moving vacuum cleaner, start doing your daily five-minute Animal Energetics sessions in the vacuum's presence when it is unplugged and quiet. Place the vacuum so that the dog can see it, its presence concerns him, but he does not become overly anxious. Practice Animal Energetics until the dog successfully ignores the vacuum at this first location. Repeat, moving the vacuum closer until finally it is next to you while you work with the dog.

Once the dog accepts the vacuum's physical presence, you can work on developing his acceptance of its noise. Turn on some quiet music and follow the same steps as above. Start with the vacuum turned on and far away. Then, move it a little closer for the next session. Repeat, until the vacuum is next to you while you work with the dog.

The next step is easy. Once the dog ignores the vacuum's noise, ask a friend or family member to move the vacuum slowly while you conduct the dog's Animal Energetics session. Follow the same steps as before. Increase the vacuum's proximity and movement until the vacuum is moving next to you and the dog remains relaxed.

This process of relaxing dogs, then exposing them to the situation that triggers their fear response can be applied to any event, object, or person. The key is to use Animal Energetics to de-stress dogs and develop their relaxation response. Building up a relaxation response causes dogs to be less sensitive to noises, objects, people, animals, and thunderstorms. When dogs are relaxed and internally quiet, they respond less intensely and ignore previously frightening situations. Whenever you and your dog encounter a new situation that threatens him, using the Animal Energetics techniques can decrease his mental, emotional, and physical stress.

House Soiling

PROBLEM IDENTIFICATION: The issue is not defecation or urination. Everyone recognizes that dogs must eliminate daily. The issue is that the dog eliminates in an inappropriate place. The problem is that the handler has not spent enough time teaching and rewarding the dog for using the correct elimination location.

KEY POINT: To recognize the dog's need to eliminate and to recognize your need for a spotless floor and carpet. To realize that your responsibility is to teach the dog where to eliminate, and consistently praise and reward the dog when he does.

RANK YOUR DOG'S HOUSE SOILING

1 = *Annoying.* The dog occasionally defecates or urinates in the house.
2 = *Serious.* The dog frequently defecates or urinates in the house.
3 = *Dangerous.* The dog has constant diarrhea, has suddenly started urinating inside the house instead of outside, or has blood in the urine and stools. (Visit your veterinarian immediately.)

TEACHING CONSIDERATIONS

1. How old is the dog? Puppies have small bladders and need to eliminate frequently. Are your expectations reasonable considering the age of the dog?
2. What type of supervision have you given the dog? Is he allowed to run free in the house without someone watching him at all times? Unsupervised dogs have more "accidents."
3. How much time have you spent with the dog to show him where he needs to eliminate? Have you worked with your dog for at least thirty days in a

row? If you have not, are your expectations reasonable considering the amount of time you have spent with the dog?

4. How long has the dog been eliminating inside the house? It takes longer to reeducate a dog who has a habit of months or years.

5. Does the dog have a health problem, for example, a urinary tract infection? Schedule a physical examination with your veterinarian to eliminate any physical problems.

6. Is your dog on any medication? Sometimes medication affects a dog's ability to control his bowel or bladder.

7. Is your dog incontinent due to old age? Older dogs have special needs and you will need to adjust your schedule and lifestyle to the dog's condition.

STRATEGIES TO CHANGE BEHAVIOR

All good things take time. This is definitely true when you teach your dog where to eliminate. In the beginning, the more time you spend with your dog, the easier it will be for him to learn. The key is to have realistic expectations. If you have a puppy and work eight hours a day, there is no way a puppy can "hold it" until you come home. Nor can most puppies last through the entire night without needing to eliminate. If you have an adolescent or older dog with an elimination problem, you will need to set up *regular* feeding times and outside elimination times, watch over him when he is inside the house, and confine him to an area when you cannot supervise him. In addition, remove the dog's water bowl one hour before bedtime. Controlling when the dog eats and drinks helps you regulate when your dog needs to eliminate.

Be proactive! Until your dog understands where he is supposed to relieve himself, you will need to devote all your available time, energy, and attention to teaching him what you expect. The good news is that most dogs can learn what is expected in a few weeks. Your responsibility is to continue rewarding your dog's daily eliminations for the rest of his life. That's right, forever. This does not mean that you will always run out to your dog with a food reward saying "good boy" as he finishes his "business." It does mean that you will watch and praise him regularly.

If you get frustrated trying to teach your dog where to eliminate, think about this: Most parents wait two or three years before they start potty training their children. On the other hand, dogs learn where to eliminate in three or four weeks if you work with them consistently, and the payback is enormous. In return for twenty-eight days of your time, you have at least ten or more years (the average life span of most dogs) of stress-free living.

The following solutions are not divided into the PAR response categories. Teaching dogs where to eliminate depends primarily on the handler's behavior. If your dog eliminates in the house, it is not the dog's fault; you have not spent enough time working with him.

SOLUTION 1—the first step. Establish a word signal and say it while the dog urinates or defecates so that the dog learns to associate the word signal with the behavior. In my house we use the words "tinkletime" and "go poop," two phrases that are not heard in daily conversation.

By pairing a word signal to a behavior, in three or four weeks, you can say "go poop," "potty time," "outside," or "do your business," and many dogs will go outside and eliminate. When the dog eliminates, praise him. Walk up to him quietly and give him a food reward. Do not wait to reward the dog until he returns to you, or he will associate the reward with returning to you and not for eliminating at the correct location.

Remember, once a dog has eliminated outside, do not immediately ask him to come back inside. Some dogs will "hold it" for as long as possible to avoid returning inside. An effective reward for a dog after he eliminates is to take him on a walk. This is a huge reward, since dogs love to go on walks. If your time is limited, play a short game of ball or Frisbee.

After a dog eliminates you can keep him with you or allow him free run in the house. The wisest course of action is always to keep the dog under close supervision until he is totally trustworthy. If you allow the dog to wander unsupervised, at least limit his access to the entire house by closing all doors to bedrooms, bathrooms, the family room, and the basement.

SOLUTION 2—the second step. Design a schedule and stick to it. You need to take puppies and dogs outdoors to eliminate on a regular basis. Puppies need to eliminate:

- After a night's sleep
- After a nap
- After feeding
- After playing

HELP

If your dog does not eliminate when you let him outside, do not allow him free run in the house when he returns. Confine him to an area such as the kitchen or utility room, or keep him with you. Take him outside again in fifteen minutes. If he eliminates, praise and reward him. If he does not, take him with you or return him to the area.

If you keep the dog with you, watch him closely. If the dog starts circling, sniffing, or goes to an area where he has eliminated before, you must take him out immediately. If you do not watch him and he eliminates, it is not his fault. It is your mistake for not paying close attention to him.

- When you come home from work
- Before going to bed in the evening
- During the night

Adult dogs have bigger bladders, but they still need to go outside after a night's sleep, after feeding, when you come home from work, and before going to sleep at night. In addition, many older dogs must be let out more frequently.

Keep a record of when your dog eliminates and what precedes it. Tack it on a cupboard or put it on your refrigerator door. For example, I played with the puppy for ten minutes at 10:15 A.M. After I finished playing, he sniffed, circled, and wet at 10:30 A.M.

You will soon notice that your dog tends to eliminate at certain times and after particular activities every day, as long as he eats at approximately the same time. By keeping track of your dog's habits, it becomes easier for you to know when to take your dog outside.

SOLUTION 3—the third step. Teach your dog to inform you when he needs to go outside to eliminate. You can teach a dog to ring a bell, fetch a certain toy and bring it to you, bark, or take you to the door. The following steps explain how to teach a dog to pick up a specific toy and bring it to you as a signal that he wants to go outside. Choose your practice times carefully. You want to build on the dog's natural inclination to eliminate at a certain time or activity.

1. Find a toy that you will use only for this purpose. My favorite toy for this activity is a fire hydrant, but any toy works fine.
2. Put the "potty toy" on the floor or wiggle it in front of the dog's nose. When the dog grabs it, say "outside" and take him out.
3. When you walk outside, take the toy from the dog. Tell him, "Outside, go potty."
4. Repeat over a number of days, until the dog associates picking up the potty toy with going outside.
5. Now, the dog must learn to bring the potty toy to you. Use the same teaching method as in the find-the-toy game on pages 240–41. When the dog brings you the potty toy, say "outside." Then, take him outside to eliminate. After a few weeks, the dog will associate picking up the toy

and bringing it to you with going outside to eliminate.

You can use this same idea to teach a dog to ring a bell or bark at the door. The secret is to connect a specific dog behavior (eliminate on signal), to an activity (fetch the toy, ring a bell, bark) with a response on your part (let the dog out).

SOLUTION 4—other options. If you cannot let your puppy out during the day due to your work schedule, hire a pet-sitter or have a friend let your puppy out at least twice during an eight-hour day. If you cannot find someone, designate a preferred potty area inside your house. You can use newspapers, doggy pads, or a doggy box (similar to a cat's litter box) to designate the correct potty space. Then, teach your dog to use this area and reward him when he does. However, realize that when they use a potty area inside the house, it usually takes longer for dogs to learn to eliminate outside.

SOLUTION 5. Install a doggy door and teach the dog how to use it, providing you have a fenced yard. If you choose this option, watch the dog after he goes through the door. When he eliminates, praise and reward him.

SOLUTION 6. Take time off from work and use your vacation days to teach the dog where to eliminate. If you cannot take vacation days, use a three- or four-day holiday to start teaching your dog the correct location.

SOLUTION 7. If you have a male dog who marks to show "territory," neuter him in addition to using the other solutions.

SOLUTION 8. If your dog only eliminates in one area inside the house, place his water bowl there. As a rule a dog will not soil an area where he eats or sleeps. You can also conduct play sessions and work sessions (sit, down, roll over) in that area so that the dog claims that area as his and will not eliminate in that space.

SOLUTION 9. If your previously well-trained dog starts having elimination problems, check with a veterinarian immediately. The dog may be sick. If it turns out that your dog does not suffer from a medical problem but is having physical problems due to old age, put the dog on an elimination schedule as you would a puppy. Understand that your older dog knows what to do, but the

---

HELP

If you see your dog eliminate in the house, redirect him. Say in a low voice "OUTSIDE!" Hopefully, the sound of your voice will interrupt him. Walk *quietly* toward the dog. Quickly take him to the door and let him out. Repeat your signal. Say "Outside! Potty!" Wait and watch the dog. Then, praise and reward him if he eliminates. After ten minutes if he does not eliminate, bring him back inside. Do not allow him free run of the house. Take your dog outside again after fifteen or twenty minutes. With adolescent or adult dogs, keep them with you or confine them in one room.

Do not hit, scream, yell, or rub your dog's nose in the "accident." You do not want your dog to fear you so that he eliminates inside the house, but only when he cannot see you. Your goal is to teach your dog *where* to eliminate, not *how* to be afraid.

conditions of age may prevent him from reaching the outdoors at the correct time.

Hyperactivity

PROBLEM IDENTIFICATION: The issue is not that the dog runs, leaps, jumps, or uses the house as a speedway. The issue is that the dog's high-energy activity level disrupts the people, children, or other animals who live in the house. The problem is that the handler has not learned how to channel the dog's energy into acceptable behaviors.

KEY POINT: To recognize that dogs are active animals who are bred to run, chase, hunt, and explore. To realize your responsibility is to channel his energy into appropriate outlets and to find ways to relax him.

RANK YOUR DOG'S ACTIVITY LEVEL

1 = *Annoying.* The dog is active and runs through the house, yips for attention, and jumps on visitors. However, when you are alone with the dog, he acts fairly calm and listens to your signals.

2 = *Serious.* The dog is extremely active and chases, follows, runs, and leaps through the house after family members, visitors, and other animals. Occasionally, the dog listens to you.

3 = *Dangerous.* The dog never stops moving, jumping, or barking. The dog chases and attacks other animals, lunges and growls at visitors, or

destroys furniture, clothes, and shoes in frantic bursts of activity. The dog ignores your signals, does not listen to you, and acts in an extremely destructive or threatening manner.

TEACHING CONSIDERATIONS

1. How old is the dog? Puppies and adolescent dogs are naturally peppy.
2. Some breeds are more active than other breeds. For example, a weimaraner is more energetic in his basic living skills than a Newfoundland.
3. Is the dog reacting to someone who lives in the house who has a nervous, frantic, angry, frustrated, or anxious personality? Is the house full of high-energy activity from young children and their friends? Is your home so active that the dog has no place to rest quietly? Younger, active children or intense, excitable, energetic adults can provide so much stimulation that dogs cannot relax. Shouting, yelling, or constant activity often increases a dog's activity level, whereas quiet, relaxed, or low-key people and activities create little stress and soothe dogs.
4. How much time does the dog spend alone every day? Is he kept outside all of the time? Is he confined in a crate or small area for long periods of time? Dogs who live outside all day long in fenced backyards, in kennel runs, or tied to trees or clotheslines cannot learn how to act calmly inside the house if they are never allowed inside or are only allowed inside for short periods of time. When dogs live outside, kids playing, wandering

cats or squirrels, cars driving by, or sirens sound-
ing can overstimulate them and increase their
anxiety level.

On the other hand, dogs who are isolated inside a crate, small area, or basement lack stimulation. This separation intensifies their anxiety,
which then exhibits itself in heightened displays
of running, jumping, spinning, or destruction.

5. Is the dog's diet affecting his behavior? The old
saying that you are what you eat applies to dogs
too. In the same way some children become more
active when they eat foods high in sugar, caffeine, or preservatives, dogs can also be affected
by what they eat. Evaluate what you feed your
dog. If you need help with this task, ask a veterinarian who specializes in diet and nutrition to
help you determine if your dog's food is easily
digestible and contains an appropriate amount of
protein, fat, carbohydrates, minerals, vitamins,
and amino acids.

6. How much physical and mental exercise does the
dog receive every day? Dogs are like kids. Children go to school to learn reading, writing, and
arithmetic. However, they also study geography,
history, music, art, and science. Teachers do not
expect their students to remain seated quietly all
day. They involve their students in physically solving problems—for example, measuring the
length of every object in the room with a ruler
when they study measurement, reading aloud, or
participating in work groups to create a bridge or
castle. In addition, class work is always interrupted by breaks for recess.

Dogs also need mental stimulation. If you engage a dog's mind in specific activities like searching and digging for hidden toys or working through mazes, the dog focuses his attention and energy on solving those problems. Once problems are solved, dogs frequently rest. Busy brains create calm bodies. Dogs require a balance between exercise, attention, mental stimulation, and calming activities.

STRATEGIES TO CHANGE BEHAVIOR

Hyperactive dogs are usually high-energy, enthusiastic, friendly, sensitive, and intelligent—the perfect dog for a companion if those characteristics are guided into appropriate behaviors. The challenge you face is to teach an active dog how to find constructive ways to express himself.

An effective method for diminishing a dog's frantic activity is Animal Energetics because it relaxes the dog's mind and body. Animal Energetics relieves physical, mental, and emotional stress. The key is to use Animal Energetics to develop your dog's relaxation response. The presence of a relaxation response changes frantic energy into quiet energy, and your dog's reactions soften and become less intense. Whenever your dog acts wildly, Animal Energetics reduces his energy with only a little effort. Turn to chapters 8 and 9 for a thorough discussion of Animal Energetics principles and practices.

Finally, practice patience. It takes time and the creation of special learning situations to develop a dog's ability to become calm, quiet, and centered. Realize that if your dog is kept outside, changing his behavior takes even longer.

If your dog has a high Mental Power Level, try this:

SOLUTION 1. Teach your dog how to sit, down, come, stay, and stand. All of these exercises require dogs to engage their minds and listen to you. Practice these behaviors with your dog every day.

SOLUTION 2. When a dog becomes active, ask him to sit, down, come, fetch, or do tricks. Have him do a series of behaviors. For example, ask him to sit, down, stand, and then repeat them in a different order. Or, ask the dog to come, sit, and wait while you throw his ball or toy. On another occasion, ask him to crawl under chairs or tables and sit by your side before you throw his toy. Use your imagination to stimulate your dog's thinking ability.

SOLUTION 3. Whenever you see your dog laying or sitting quietly, praise him and introduce any word or phrase that means "chill out." For example, "Good Buffy," "Good girl," "Chill out," "Good chill." Give Buffy a food treat if you have one with you, or reward her with a Soft Breeze (pages 192–97). Also, during any Animal Energetics session when the dog relaxes completely, tell him "chill out."

SOLUTION 4. Teach your dog to chill out on signal. In the same way you teach dogs how to sit, come, or stay, you can teach them how to settle down or rest quietly. Chill out does not mean your dog sits or lies immobile on the floor in a perfect stay. Chill out means that the dog stays primarily in one location, but he can shift positions. He can roll on his back, lie on his side, sit, or scratch, as long as he does so quietly.

To teach your dog how to chill out, practice the following steps during times when there are as few distractions and activities as possible inside your house. An easy time to practice this is during commercial breaks while you watch television.

Step 1. Begin by asking your dog to pay attention to you. Turn to pages 114–18 to learn how to teach your dog to focus.

Step 2. As the dog waits and watches, praise him. Do not feed or touch him; use only verbal praise. At this point the dog will not understand what he is doing that is earning your praise. He may bring you a toy. If he does, ignore it.

Step 3. Tell the dog while he waits to chill out. You want him to learn that when you say "chill out," playtime is over and quiet time has arrived. Build up

HELP
If the dog stares at you, barks, or nuzzles you with his nose, turn your head and avert your eyes. Repeat again "chill out." Breathe deeply. Your body language tells the dog that you do not want to play with him now. At this point he may stand, sit, or lie down. If he does, praise him. If he moves away from you and lies down, praise him.

the time you ask the dog to chill out slowly. Start with ten seconds and build to twenty seconds, forty-five seconds, and a minute and more.

Step 4. Teach your dog a second signal that means he can move around again, such as "up-and-at-it" or "free." Remember, keep realistic expectations. Dogs, like children, need recess.

If your dog has a high Physical Activity Level, try this:

SOLUTION 5. Use the playSMART approach and teach your "take-charge" or high-energy dog the search game. For a description of the search game, see page 243.

SOLUTION 6. Hire a pet-sitter or ask a friend to take your dog on a work-time walk if you will be gone for eight hours or more. For additional information about work-time walks turn to page 89.

SOLUTION 7. If you have not taught your dog how to chill out on signal and you need a break, give you and your dog a short, ten-minute-or-less time-out. Putting your dog in a different room away from you gives you and your dog a chance to start over in a few minutes when you both feel refreshed.

SOLUTION 8. Close the drapes, curtains, or blinds so the sight-sensitive dog cannot see what is happening outside. If you do not want to shutter the entire house, keep the dog in a room that can be sheltered from distractions while you are away.

SOLUTION 9. Play soft music or talk radio to cover outside noises that upset your noise-sensitive dog.

SOLUTION 10. Teach your children how to act around movement-, noise-, and sight-sensitive dogs. If your children are running and playing in the backyard and you see that their frenzied activity upsets the dog, bring the dog inside. In addition, teach your children how to play fetch and find-me games, or have hug, snuggle, and pet sessions with the dogs. Do not let them play chase, tug, or pull games with dogs. Never leave children and dogs together unsupervised.

SOLUTION 11. Change the dog from being an outside dog to an inside dog when you are gone. If you are worried about chewing or house soiling while you are away, turn to pages 238–45 and 258–67.

If your dog has a high Emotional Response Level, try this:

SOLUTION 12. Overactive dogs frequently store stress in their mouths, paws, legs, and rear ends. During your daily five-minute Animal Energetics session, form Mountains on the dog's legs and Lakes on his paws and rear end. Make sure you turn his tail into a Rainbow. For the Mountain, Lake, and Rainbow techniques turn to chapter 9.

SOLUTION 13. Hyper dogs also store tension in their mouths. Do at least three 10-second Cave sessions every day, and de-stress your dog's mouth. For the Cave technique turn to pages 208–12.

SOLUTION 14. Before you leave home, use Soft Breezes and perform the 10-second Leaving Routine to decrease your dog's anxieties. Turn to page 216 for a description of the "Leaving Routine."

Ignores You

PROBLEM IDENTIFICATION: The issue is not that dogs ignore handlers. The issue is that you feel frustrated, annoyed, rejected, or angry when your dog does not do what you want. The problem is that you have not learned how to effectively communicate with the dog.

KEY POINT: To recognize that your dog has separate interests from yours. To realize that your responsibility is to stimulate and direct the dog's attention to you, and provide the dog with the correct schooling environment.

RANK YOUR DOG'S INATTENTION

1 = *Annoying.* The dog occasionally listens to you when you tell him "no," "off," "chill out," "sit," "down," or "come," but not all the time.

2 = *Serious.* The dog rarely listens to you, and does whatever he wants to do, in spite of your instructions.

3 = *Dangerous.* The dog never listens to you, and willfully attacks, destroys, or runs away.

TEACHING CONSIDERATIONS

1. Do you expect your dog to follow orders like a mechanical robot? Dogs have ideas and interests separate from their handlers. Successful teaching requires that you design schooling sessions that build on a dog's natural interests and gifts. Dogs cannot learn as easily if their environment is full

of distractions such as playing children, people talking, wandering animals, or scattered toys and balls.

2. Have you taught the dog to look to you for direction and to listen to what you say? How often do you repeat your behavior signal? Do you say "sit" once and wait five seconds for the dog to respond? Your dog's ability to learn hinges on your ability as a teacher. Teaching a dog to pay attention to you requires that you pay attention to your dog and develop teaching skills that stimulate and maintain his interest in you and your signals. Do not expect your dog to be a good student if you have not mastered good teaching skills.

3. Do you reward your dog when he responds, or do you take his response for granted? Dogs, like people, perform better when they are noticed, praised, and rewarded. No one likes to receive constant criticism. If all your dog hears you say is "no," "quit," "off," and "stop," he will tune you out. Remember, *catch a dog doing something right*. And what do you do when you catch him? Reward him.

4. What tone of voice do you use with your dog? Is it too quiet, soft, loud, or abrasive? Your tone of voice and the amount of enthusiasm you display affects a dog's ability to listen.

STRATEGIES TO CHANGE BEHAVIOR

How would you describe your favorite television show? Action? Adventure? Comedy? Drama? Have you ever changed channels when a program was boring or dull? A dog's ability to focus on his handler depends on the handler's ability to keep up the dog's interest and enthusiasm for listening and following directions. No one leaves the room during the fourth quarter of the Super Bowl if the score is tied. No one decides to mow the yard and miss the last half-hour of a riveting action movie. Dogs do not ignore handlers who are more interesting, exciting, and fun than the surrounding environment.

If your dog has a high Mental Power Level, try this:

SOLUTION 1. Teach your dog how to sit, down, come, stay, and stand. All of these exercises require dogs to engage their brain and listen to you. Practice these signals with your dog every day.

SOLUTION 2. Anytime your dog looks at you or watches you, praise him.

SOLUTION 3. Show your dog in subtle ways that you expect respect. For example, walk through doors first, feed the dog after you eat, have the dog sit before feeding him. You determine when a play session begins and ends, not your dog. If the dog nuzzles your arm to have you pet him, make him earn your attention by requiring him to sit or lie down before you pet him.

SOLUTION 4. Keep your dog's interest. Make teaching sessions fun. Do not repeat the same lesson over and over. If the dog loses interest, do something unexpected to return his attention to you—for example, lie on the ground, dig a hole, walk on your knees, hold your hands above your head and spin, sit down, turn your back, or squeak a toy.

SOLUTION 5. Play games such as fetch or find me that reward dogs for paying attention to you. Act enthusiastic. Change the expression of your voice. Whistle, shout, jump up and down, or whisper. Dogs want to have fun, so playSMART! For more playSMART ideas, see chapter 5.

If your dog has a high Physical Activity Level, try this:

SOLUTION 6. When you ask your "take-charge" and high-energy dog to do something, give him time to respond (five seconds) before you repeat the signal. When he responds, praise and reward him.

If the dog ignores a behavior signal, use a different technique that draws his attention to your request. For example, if you ask him to sit and he does not sit, use a food treat and lure him into sitting quickly.

SOLUTION 7. If your dog sails by you when you call him, use the playSMART approach and teach your dog the "human tunnel" game. Then, the dog will learn to come directly to you. Use the following steps:

Step 1. Say "come."

Step 2. While the dog is close enough to see you, but still far enough away so that he has not veered away from you, throw a toy, ball, or dog biscuit between your open legs.

Step 3. Watch as the dog zooms through your legs in order to get the item. Repeat.

Step 4. Once the dog zooms through your open legs,

say "come." Close your legs and reward the dog when he stops in front you.

SOLUTION 8. If a dog ignores you when you say "no," use a different technique such as a squirt of water on his nose to get his attention. Then, use a redirection.

SOLUTION 9. Change the environment. Is the sight-, sound-, noise-, and movement-sensitive dog distracted because you are trying to teach him to walk quietly in a busy park? Are you working on come when children are playing nearby? Find quiet times to work with your dog. Then, when the dog understands a specific signal, increase the number of distractions or change the location.

If your dog has a high Emotional Response Level, try this:

SOLUTION 10. Practice Animal Energetics and teach your dog that your hands (and presence) bring him relief, comfort, and attention.

Jumping

PROBLEM IDENTIFICATION: The issue is not that dogs jump. The issue is that the dog does not know how to interact with people, children, household items, or furniture. The problem is you have not taught the dog what to do instead of jumping.

KEY POINT: To recognize that dogs need contact and display exuberance, and to recognize your desire to keep high-energy physical encounters to a minimum. To realize that your responsibility is to teach dogs how to conduct themselves with people and objects.

RANK YOUR DOG'S JUMPING

1 = *Annoying.* The dog jumps on family members and visitors only when they walk in the house. Occasionally, the dog jumps on furniture or the bed.

2 = *Serious.* The dog jumps on family members and visitors when they walk in the house, while they hold food in their hands, or if someone talks on the phone. The dog also jumps on furniture or beds, grabs pillows, and brings them to other locations in the house. The dog jumps and eats food off the counters, or snatches food out of people's hands.

3 = *Dangerous.* The dog jumps, lunges, growls, and attacks.

TEACHING CONSIDERATIONS

1. Did you or a member of your household allow a puppy to jump up in greeting or play? Puppies grow into adult dogs, and what is "cute" in a puppy often becomes an undesirable trait in an adult dog.

2. Have you or other family members increased your dog's jumping and agitation by enthusiastically greeting or playing with the dog when you first arrive home? These actions strengthen a dog's jumping response. They do not reduce it.

3. Is everyone consistent in their response to the dog's jumping? Or, do some people or children encourage the dog to jump up? Do you ever invite your puppy or dog up on a couch with you? You cannot have two different sets of rules. For example, you cannot invite the dog to share the couch with you while you watch television if you do not want the dog on the couch when you are not home. Teach household members that jumping is not permitted as a dog greeting. In addition, explain that everyone must greet the dog calmly when they have been absent.

STRATEGIES TO CHANGE BEHAVIOR

I want my dogs to like me and to miss my presence. If I came home and my dogs looked up, saw me, and walked away, I would be very unhappy. However, I do not want to feel like I am in the middle of a combat zone when I enter the house. For me, returning home is one of the best parts of my day. Red Sun Rising rushes up and sits four feet from the door, eagerly awaiting his welcome-home rubs. Trevor, the twelve-year-old, lays in place, waiting for me to come over and greet him. I love family reunions whether I have been away two hours, three days, or two weeks.

Teaching a dog how to greet you is fun. You can teach your dog how to sit-stay, how to bring a toy to you, or how to direct his energy into running to the room you will enter next. When dogs learn they earn more praise and attention when they sit instead of jump to greet you, their jumping vanishes.

If your dog has a high Mental Response Level, try this:

SOLUTION 1. Use the playSMART approach and redirect your dog's energy into the find-the-toy game. Turn to pages 240–41 to learn how to teach this game.

Upon entering the house, before you touch the dog say "find your toy." As soon as the dog brings you the toy, reward him and play with him. It will not take long before the dog learns to greet you at the door with a toy in his mouth. Asking the dog to greet you this way will channel any anticipation, anxiety, or frantic energy into searching for the toy. In all probability, the dog will chew on the toy while he waits for you to come home.

SOLUTION 2. Teach your dog he must sit before you will touch him.

SOLUTION 3. Praise and reward the dog anytime he does not jump in spite of reasons to jump. For example, if a friend comes over and the dog does not jump on her, praise and reward the dog.

SOLUTION 4. If the dog jumps on you, ignore him. Signal the dog with your body that you will not pay attention to him. Turn your head and step back quickly so that the dog's weight and gravity return him to the

HELP
If the dog keeps jumping on you, use a squirt of water to reinforce your "off" signal. As soon as the dog's feet touch the floor, reward him. Avoid squirting into the dog's eyes.

ground. Do not speak to the dog. The dog wants your attention. Pay attention to the dog only when his four feet rest on the floor. Frequently, when dogs do not receive recognition, they stop jumping.

SOLUTION 5. Teach the concept of "off." If the dog jumps on you, say "off" and back up one or two steps so that gravity returns the dog's paws to the ground. If the dog's paws remain on the floor, praise and reward him. Then, redirect him. Say "go find your toy." If the dog jumps again, repeat your previous actions.

Once your dog no longer jumps on you, set up a practice session with a friend so that the dog learns that jumping is not permitted on anyone.

If your dog has a high Physical Activity Level, try this:

SOLUTION 6. If your "take-charge" or high-energy dog jumps on furniture while you are away, limit the area that your dog has to roam in the house while you are gone. Close the doors to your bedrooms, living room, or office.

SOLUTION 7. Do not leave food out on the kitchen counters or table. Then, the presence of food will not tempt your dog to jump.

SOLUTION 8. If your movement- and sound-sensitive dog continues to jump on counters or furniture when you are not home, you can booby-trap them. Do not booby-trap your whole house. Choose one area to work with at a time. For a description of booby traps, see pages 244–45.

Once the dog stops jumping on a booby-trapped area, do not remove the cans all at once. Over a period of thirty days, place fewer and fewer cans on the counter's edge until eventually the presence of one can becomes a visual signal to the dog that indicates no jumping is allowed. Then, remove the final can on the thirtieth day.

If your dog has a high Emotional Response Level, try this:

SOLUTION 9. Tap the dog's toes frequently throughout the day to ground him.

SOLUTION 10. When the dog greets you quietly, reward that behavior with Lakes and Soft Breezes along his back, neck, and head. You will find this relaxes the dog even more, until eventually he welcomes you home by laying on his back or side to facilitate your touching.

Leash Pulling

PROBLEM IDENTIFICATION: The issue is not that dogs pull, strain, or tug against something. We want dogs to play with their toys, with us, or pull a sled or cart. However, pulling becomes a problem when dogs resist their handlers' attempts to "reel them in." The problem is that handlers have not learned how to direct their dogs' attention and strength without using muscle power.

KEY POINT: To recognize that dogs love to pull against someone or something, and to recognize your need for the dog to cooperate with you. To realize that your responsibility is to use your mind instead of your muscles when working with the dog.

RANK YOUR DOG'S LEASH PULLING

1 = *Annoying.* The dog takes you for a walk. He leads and you follow, but you are not experiencing any significant physical discomfort during your walks.

2 = *Serious.* The dog pulls you everywhere. He goes wherever he wants to, in spite of your instructions. As a result, your shoulders, hands, or back hurt.

3 = *Dangerous.* The dog lunges ahead and changes directions so quickly you have fallen down or injured your hands, wrists, shoulders, or back.

TEACHING CONSIDERATIONS

1. Does your dog understand that you are the coach and he is the player in your daily interactions? For example, if you and your dog reach a doorway together, who goes first? Does the dog sleep with you in bed? Who eats first? Dogs who pull on their leashes often believe they are the leader and you are the follower. If you allow dogs to "lead" while you are at home, they also "lead" on walks.

2. How much time have you spent working with your dog? If your dog pulls, review the basics— focus, sit, down, and come. In order for dogs to walk with you, they must know how to listen to you.

3. Does your dog listen to you at home? If the dog ignores you at home, he will not listen to you in a new location. Teach your dog how to walk qui-

etly at home before you expect him to walk, without pulling, down the street or at the park. Remember, each location may take a number of visits before the dog walks without pulling.

4. How many times have you taken your dog to unfamiliar places such as parks, beaches, or stores? The first few times dogs see anything new, it distracts them. However, if you continue to expose dogs to different surroundings, they will handle it much easier when in the presence of something "new."

5. Do you confine your dog all day in a crate, kennel, house, or backyard and then expect him to walk quietly? Always release a dog's pent-up energy before you go on a walk. Dogs who have been confined all day need an opportunity to run, jump, and play before they go for a "quiet" walk in the neighborhood or park.

6. Can you touch your dog anywhere on his body? Often, dogs who pull on their leashes have "untouchable" areas on their bodies. Examine your dog. Remember, check his "Cave" and "Rainbow," since those are two areas where dogs store a lot of tension. Turn to chapter 9 for information about the Animal Energetics Cave and Rainbow techniques.

STRATEGIES TO CHANGE BEHAVIOR

Watch dogs play with a rope toy as they pull against each other. The more one dog resists, the harder the other dog pulls. Dogs love to pull. To dogs, pulling is not a test of willpower; it is a test of strength. As dogs resist, sustained physical exertion stimulates their bodies, hormones, and "take-no-prisoners" attitude. If you try to force dogs to slow down by maintaining a steady pressure on the leash during a walk, dogs pull more. In addition, leash pulling is correlated to status. If your dog views himself as leader of the pack, his leadership position dictates that he must be out in front to survey the territory, issue challenges, or look for prey. Your task as the dog's handler is to ask the dog to join forces with you, not against you.

Your heart tells you that walking your dog is fun, good exercise, lets you meet new people, and check out different neighborhoods. However, your body reminds you that the muscle strain you feel in your arms could cause carpal tunnel syndrome in your wrists. Your mind tells you there has to be a better way to handle this tugging, sniffing, drooling, lunging dog. And there is. Practice the different solutions and discover that all leashes are not created equal; a relaxed leash is definitely the best.

If your dog has a high Mental Power Level, try this:

SOLUTION 1. Prevent your dog from pulling by walking a few steps and then asking him to sit or down. For example, walk three steps; sit. Walk four steps; sit. Walk five steps; down. Walk three steps; sit. Walk two steps; down. Walk four steps; sit and down.

SOLUTION 2. Teach the dog to watch you by changing directions frequently. Walk three steps north. Walk

HELP

If the dog forges away from you, move in the opposite direction from where he is going. For example, if the dog veers to the left, go right. However, if the dog starts to charge in front of you, cut him off by turning quickly to the left (this maneuver works only if the dog walks on your left side), or do an about-face and walk in the opposite direction. The dog will slow down to prevent himself from running into you.

eight steps south. Back up six steps. Stand still for five seconds. Walk five steps west. Circle to the east. Circle to the west. As long as the dog walks quietly with you, you can continue to increase the number of steps you walk in one direction. If the increased distance causes the dog to forge ahead and forget your presence, change directions more frequently again. Vary your speed. Practice walking at slow, fast, and normal rates.

SOLUTION 3. During your daily routine, establish in subtle ways that you are the coach and he is the player. At doorways, walk through the door before your dog. Eat before your dog eats. If your dog nuzzles you with his nose for attention, ask him to sit before you pet him. You decide when to start and stop playing. If your dog sleeps with you in bed, have him sleep on the floor next to you instead.

If your dog has a high Physical Activity Level,
try this:

SOLUTION 4. Use a playSTICK to focus your movement- and sight-sensitive dog's attention. Turn to pages 132–142 to learn how to use a playSTICK.

SOLUTION 5. Frequently, sight-sensitive dogs become easily distracted. Introduce your dog to walking on a leash *inside* your house when there are no distractions present. *Do not move* to a new location until you can maintain your dog's attention inside. Then, move to your backyard. Before you move to a new location, use dog toys, treats, friends, or family members to act as distractions.

SOLUTION 6. Teach your dog how to "backup" on signal. That way, if the dog starts to forge ahead, you can say "back." Backing stops a dog's forward motion and redirects his attention to you. To teach your dog how to back, practice the following steps inside your house in a quiet location:

Step 1. Begin by asking the dog to pay attention to you. Turn to pages 114–118 to learn how to teach your dog to focus.

Step 2. Stand with the dog on your left side. Hold a small dog biscuit in your left hand in front of the dog's nose. (Place it between your thumb and index finger.)

Step 3. Place your right hand on the point of the dog's right shoulder.

Step 4. At the same time, step back with your left foot, push on the dog's right shoulder, and say

HELP

If your dog moves forward while practicing back, move to a new location where you can face a wall. This prevents the dog from moving forward.

If your dog moves back but swings his body to the side, practice this exercise in a hallway so that the side that the dog swings wide is blocked by the wall.

"back." When the dog moves one foot back, reward him instantly. Repeat.

If your dog has a high Emotional Response Level, try this:

SOLUTION 7. Before you go on a walk with your dog, do a five-minute Animal Energetics session, since a relaxed dog is less likely to pull.

SOLUTION 8. If your dog stores tension in his mouth, do at least three 10-second Cave sessions every day and de-stress his mouth. For the Cave technique turn to pages 208–12.

SOLUTION 9. If your dog stores tension in his tail, do at least three one-minute Rainbow sessions every day and reduce his anxieties. For the Rainbow technique turn to pages 212–15.

CHAPTER 11

FRIENDS FOR LIFE

Nine years, three months, and twenty days ago Amanda, my golden retriever, died on a blue-and-white tile kitchen floor in Boston, Massachusetts. Amanda. Even with daily brushing her coat always looked rumpled. Now, it was smooth, as if on this last journey the entry had smoothed the rough, curly red coat.

What does it mean "friends for life" when your best friend lies dead in your arms and your tears explode like a dam bursting its concrete holdings?

In the beginning I could only comprehend the physical events that filled the interval between her birth and death. As a puppy Amanda attended graduate school classes with me. As a young dog, she accompanied me on my first trip to the neighborhood bar. Amanda sat next to the barstool while I talked with the patrons. When I purchased my first car, a yellow Volkswagen Rabbit, Amanda helped me inspect each car and then sat patiently as the salesman and I negotiated terms.

We shared shopping trips to the mall, breakups with boyfriends, ball games, nightly walks, even my honeymoon. Now, it was over, and the hole in my heart was the size of the Grand Canyon.

Friends for life? "But she is dead," I wailed. Only later did I realize the gifts Amanda gave me continue through today.

Amanda did not walk into my life, she ran, jumped, and leaped into it during a February blizzard. At least once a day she raced through the house like a greyhound chasing a rabbit. One circle, two circles, three, then she zipped to my feet, shook herself, and waited to see where I was going next so she could beat me there. Like a red tulip growing through a Minnesota snowbank, Amanda animated me with her zest for life and stimulated my awareness. She helped me regain the ability to listen, understand, and love, abilities I had lost or buried. When I watched her jumping as easily for a bird in the sky as diving for a rock at the bottom of the lake, I realized she represented *carpe diem*, seize the day, at its finest.

All dogs offer gifts to us. We, as their caretakers, can choose to accept or ignore them. Two simple rules can guide you if you want to develop a friendship that will change your life.

RULE #1: LISTEN TO THE DOG

> "Lots of people talk to animals," said Pooh.
> "Maybe, but . . ."
> "Not very many listen, though," he said.
> "That's the problem," he added.
> —quoted from *Winnie-the-Pooh* by A. A. Milne
> in *The Tao of Pooh* by Benjamin Hoff

Working with dogs demands that you learn how to listen with your heart, mind, ears, hands, nose, and mouth. Listening keeps you from getting stuck or confused about your dog's behavior because it helps you figure out the reasons that cause the actions. Your task is to observe closely what you see, feel, and experience.

The more you listen, the more you get past superficial responses and into the reasons behind the dog's behavior. Listening allows you to notice messages that were previously hidden from you. It teaches you to become aware of the feelings or opinions that a dog expresses through his eyes, body language, and activities.

When you listen, avoid using labels or stereotypes to describe a situation such as "All Australian shepherds bark too much" or "My West Highland white terrier is neurotic." Instead, ask questions and watch your dog to determine the answers. To understand what causes a dog's behavior, you need to layer detail upon detail until the experience is completely described. Do not assume you know the reasons for a particular behavior. For example, determine what time of day your Australian shepherd barks, what causes him to bark, if he barks inside, outside, or inside and outside, and how often he barks. Careful observations will show you why your dog barks. Once you unmask the reasons that cause the barking behavior, you can address them.

Listening also requires that you pay attention to your actions. By noticing what you do and how your dog responds, you can understand how your relationship with a dog affects the outcome. If you notice your dog only when he barks, he will bark more because he wants your attention.

Listening requires an open mind that does not jump to conclusions but views, sifts, and weighs all the evidence before making a decision. It teaches you to look at what causes a behavior instead of focusing on its symptoms.

RULE #2: TEACH YOUR DOG TO LISTEN TO YOU

In the same way you must listen to your dog, your dog needs to listen to you. The issue is not control; it's communication. Fortunately, dogs want to listen to us.

A dog's unique ability to think aids, not hinders, the learning process. When you establish yourself as the link between what dogs think and how they act, you can help them make decisions based on more than instinct. Your aim is that the dog pauses before he acts, and during that pause, he looks to you for advice.

Every lesson you teach develops the link between you and your dog. You teach your dog to focus, sit, down, stay, come, or stand not because you want an obedience champion but to use these exercises to teach listening skills. Then, when Aunt Mildred comes to visit, you can ask the dog to down-stay, and he cannot jump on her. He cannot race out the door when you open it to buy Girl Scout cookies, and he cannot beg at the dinner table. When your dog listens to any signal you send, behavior problems disappear.

These two rules form the basis for a successful relationship between you and your dog. The reason is simple. When you both develop the ability to listen, you increase your sensitivity to each other. If you send a message, you know the dog receives it; and if the dog gives you a message, you are open to it. If you are lucky, as time passes something magical happens between you and your dog.

When we accepted the dog's presence at our campfire, we accepted more than caring for his physical needs; we accepted his love. Love is a funny word—so inadequate to describe the feeling I get when Trevor looks at me, head up, a relaxed grin stretching his mouth until his lower jaw drops to take up the slack; or when I see Red racing through the yard leaping over jumps, tunneling through tires, flushing out quails and cats; or when I feel them sleeping next to me, lulling me with their gentle, rhythmic breathing. When dogs enter our lives, they begin a journey that leads straight to our hearts.

Amanda taught me that she and I were born with only half a heart. When she entered my life, her spirit, animation, and joy filled my heart and opened it to hers. Over time, love glued our two heart-halves together. Now I know that everyone is born with only half a heart, that we remain isolated but for the love of a dog.

Trevor and Red rest quietly at my feet. They seem oblivious to my gaze. Yet, I know in another instant Trevor or Red will raise his head, and our eyes and hearts will blend together. Finally, I understand this gift of life that dogs bring to the empty places and hidden spaces in a person's heart. With a dog you are never alone.

Appendix A

ANIMAL ENERGETICS TECHNIQUES FOR SPECIFIC PROBLEMS						
Behavior Problem	*Soft Breezes*	*Lakes*	*Mountains*	*Rainbows*	*Caves*	*Leaving Routine*
Barking	🐾	🐾		🐾	🐾	🐾
Biting	🐾	🐾		🐾	🐾	🐾
Chewing	🐾	🐾			🐾	🐾
Digging		🐾	🐾	🐾	🐾	🐾
Fear responses	🐾	🐾		🐾	🐾	🐾
Ignores you	🐾	🐾	🐾			
Jumping	🐾	🐾	🐾	🐾		
Hyperactivity	🐾	🐾	🐾	🐾	🐾	🐾
Leash pulling	🐾		🐾	🐾	🐾	
Physical Problem						
Aching	🐾	🐾	🐾		🐾	
Breathing	🐾	🐾	🐾	🐾	🐾	
Bruising	🐾	🐾				
Congestion	🐾	🐾	🐾		🐾	
Excess heat	🐾	🐾			🐾	
Overexertion	🐾	🐾			🐾	
Stiffness	🐾	🐾	🐾	🐾	🐾	
Sprains	🐾	🐾	🐾			
Swelling	🐾	🐾	🐾			

Appendix B
EQUIPMENT

Based on my experiences with a variety of dogs and their problems, the following list describes the basic training tools available and my preferences.

Collars

There are three basic collar styles: choke chains, flat nylon or leather collars, and harnesses. I recommend using a flat collar or a harness when you work with your dog.

Choke collars are used by handlers who believe they are required to control a dog's body. With the body-MIND approach for teaching dogs, choke collars are unnecessary. Indeed, choke chains can cause muscle and tissue damage when used incorrectly. Also, if choke chains get caught on something such as a branch, fence, or carpet loop, the dog's air can be cut off, and the dog can strangle.

Flat collars allow connection with the dog's neck, but they cannot contrict it. When you are not with the dog, flat collars should be fastened loose enough so that if the collar catches on something, the dog can slip out of it.

Flexible harnesses connect the dog's neck and body. However, they should not be left on a dog continuously because they can also get caught. Harnesses avoid potential injuries to a dog's neck and do not choke dogs.

Leashes

There are four primary leash materials: chain, nylon, cloth, or leather. I recommend using leather or cotton leashes when you work with your dog. For me, chain leashes make noise and can be difficult to hold. Nylon leashes are flexible. However, they can "burn" your hands if the leash runs through them quickly. Leather or cotton leashes are flexible and easy on hands.

The length of leashes varies. Most of the time a six-foot leash is all you will need. A six-foot leash allows you to keep your dog close to you. Tab leashes are short, eight- to twelve-inch leashes that are useful when you introduce off-leash work, work dogs through tunnels and over jumps, or are in a situation where your dog must stay very close to you. Long lines are approximately twenty feet and are perfect for teaching "come."

Index